2ND EDITION

FOR ORGANS, PIANOS & ELECTRONIC KEYBOARDS

E-Z PLAY® TODAY

111

Season's Greetings

T0034077

ISBN-13: 978-0-6340-1828-2

HAL•LEONARD® CORPORATION

7777 W. BLUEMOUND RD. P.O. BOX 13819 MILWAUKEE, WI 53213

Visit Hal Leonard Online at
www.halleonard.com

Season's Greetings

All I Want for Christmas Is You

Registration 5
Rhythm: Swing

Words and Music by Mariah Carey
and Walter Afanasieff

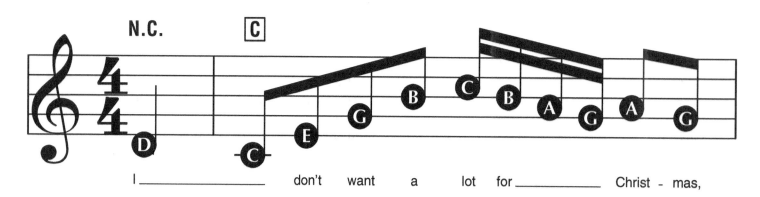

I _____ don't want a lot for _____ Christ - mas,

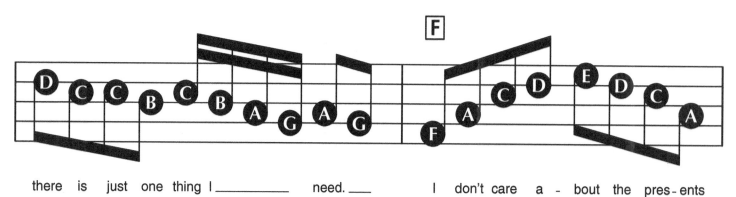

there is just one thing I _____ need. ___ I don't care a - bout the pres - ents

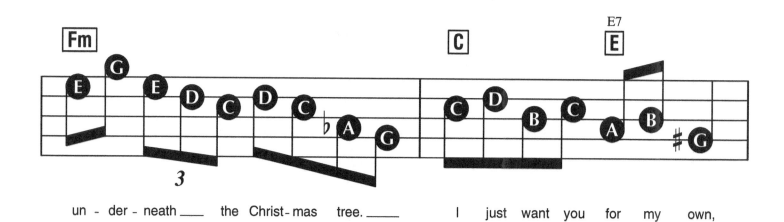

un - der - neath ___ the Christ - mas tree. ___ I just want you for my own,

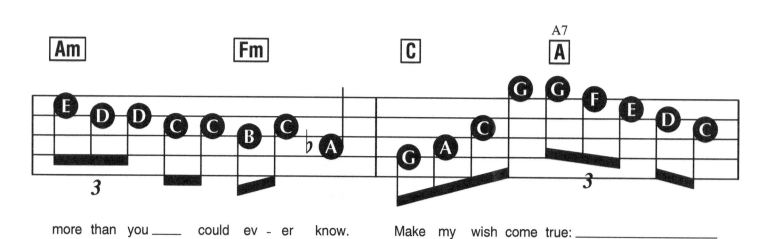

more than you ___ could ev - er know. Make my wish come true: _____

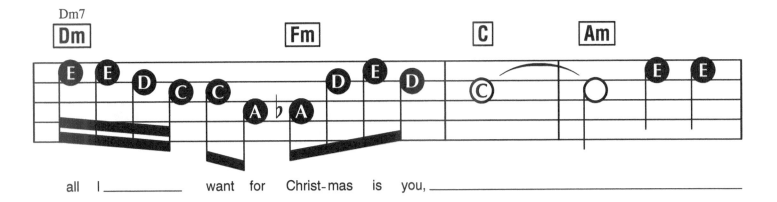

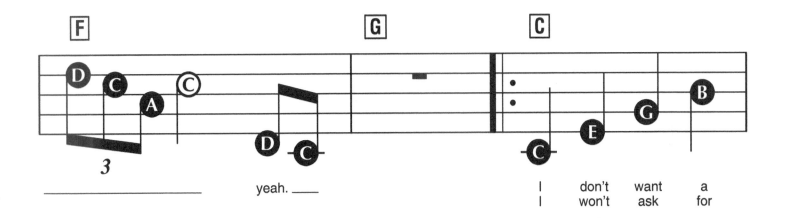

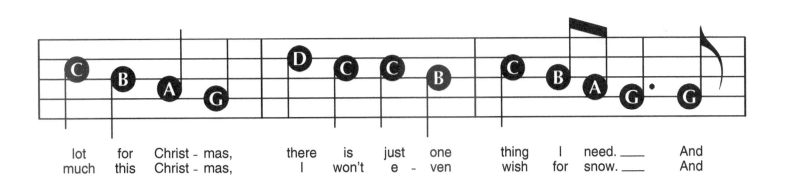

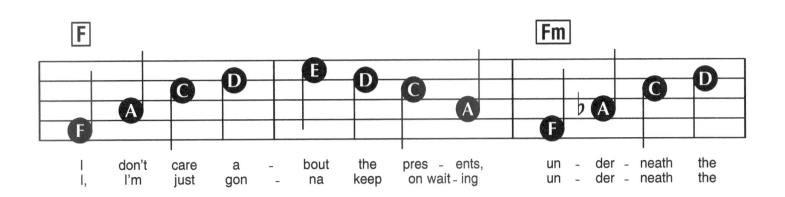

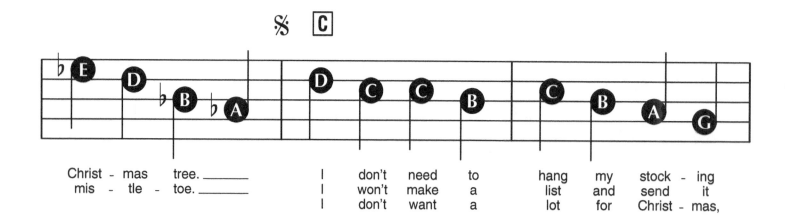

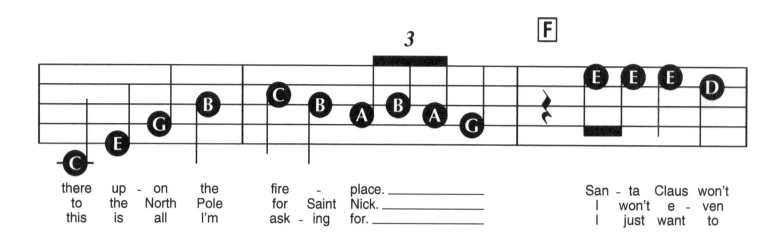

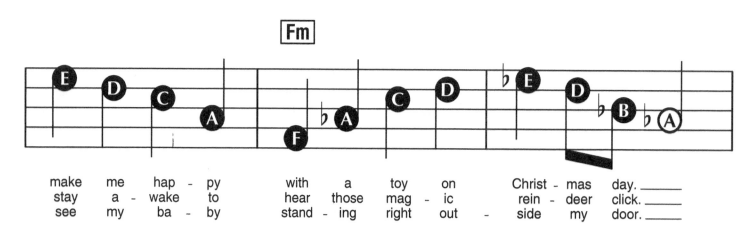

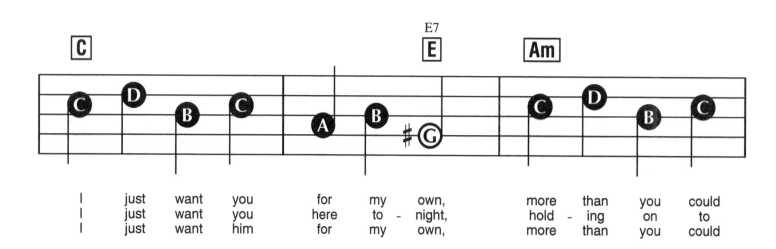

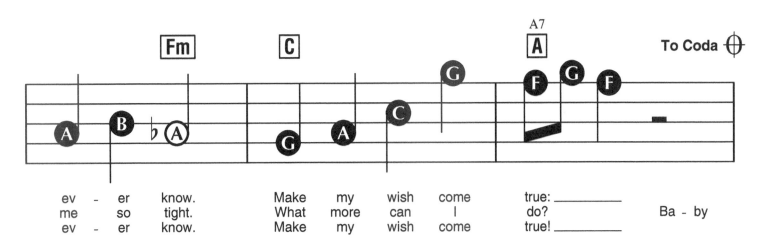

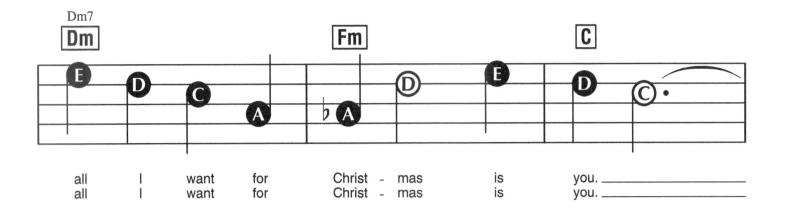

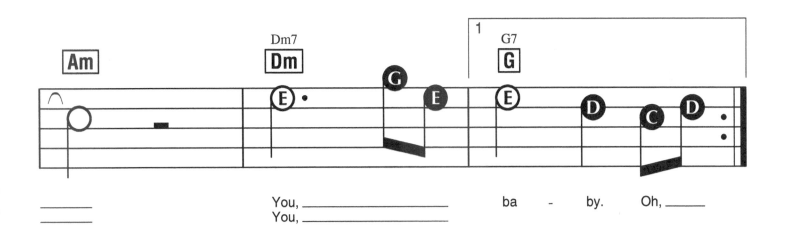

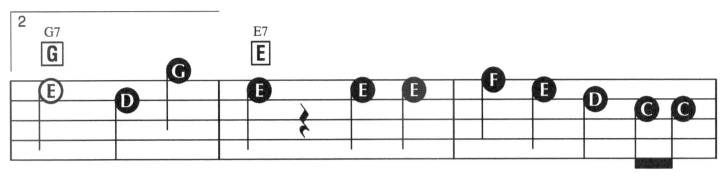

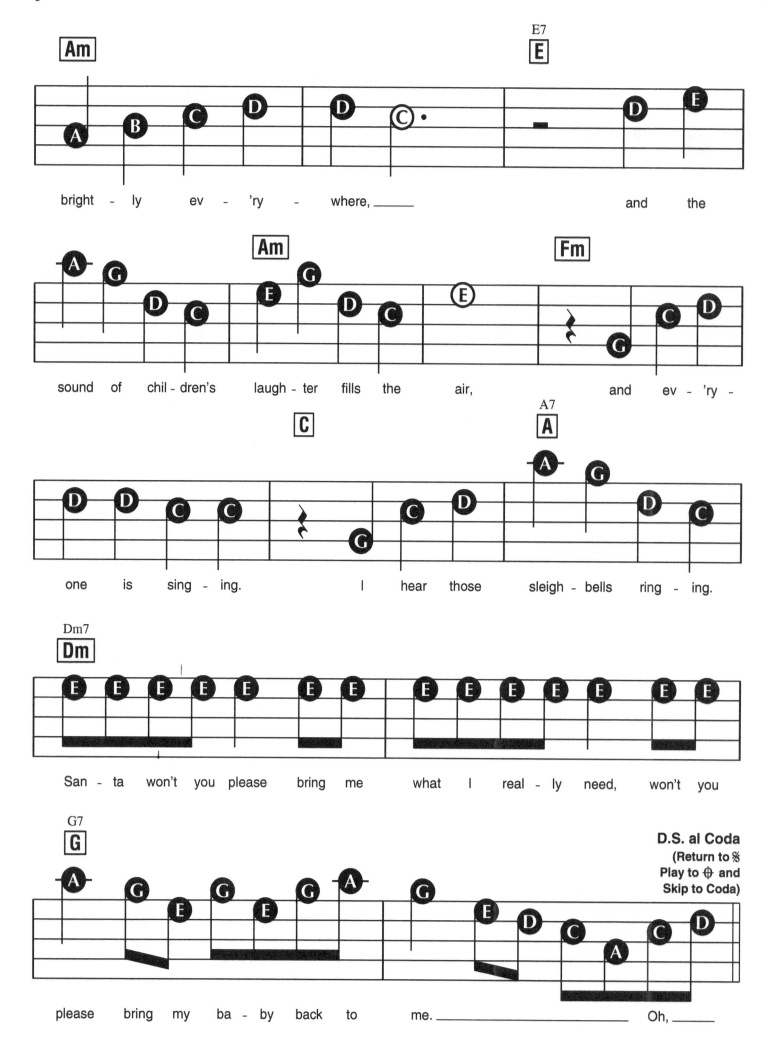

9

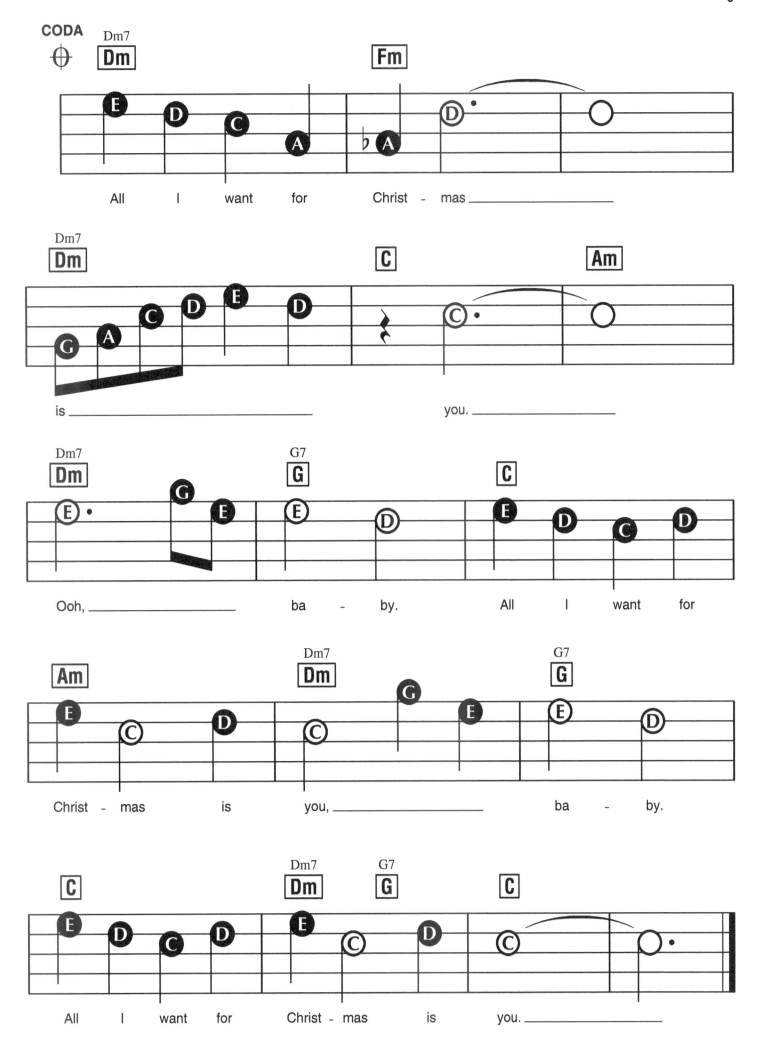

As Long as There's Christmas
from Walt Disney's
BEAUTY AND THE BEAST - THE ENCHANTED CHRISTMAS

Registration 3
Rhythm: Waltz

Music by Rachel Portman
Lyrics by Don Black

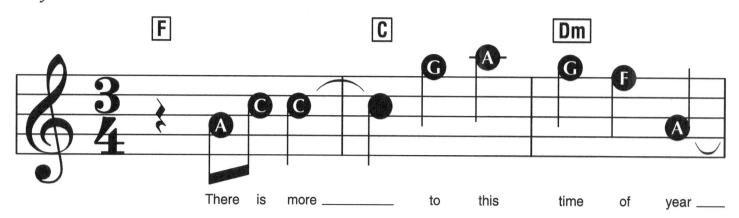

There is more _____ to this time of year _____

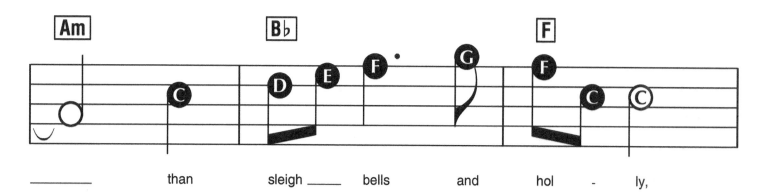

_____ than sleigh ____ bells and hol - ly,

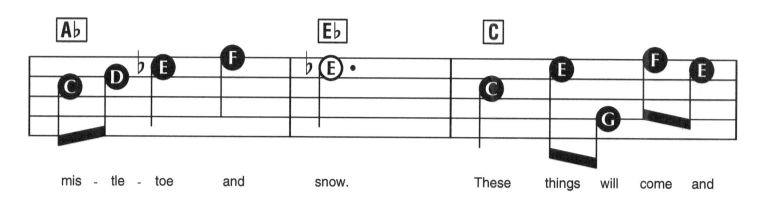

mis - tle - toe and snow. These things will come and

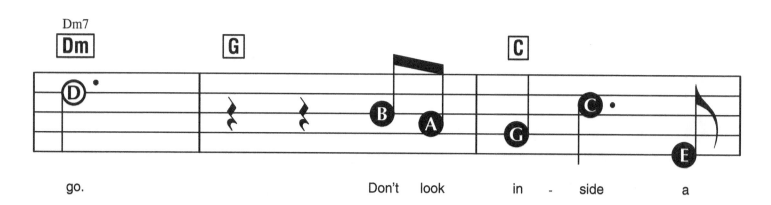

go. Don't look in - side a

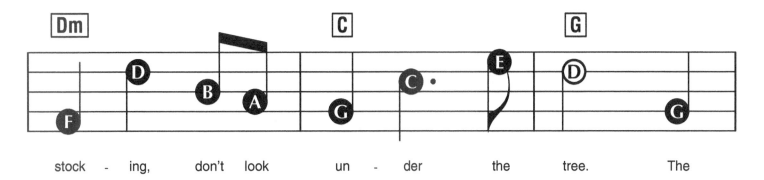

stock - ing,   don't   look   un - der   the   tree.   The

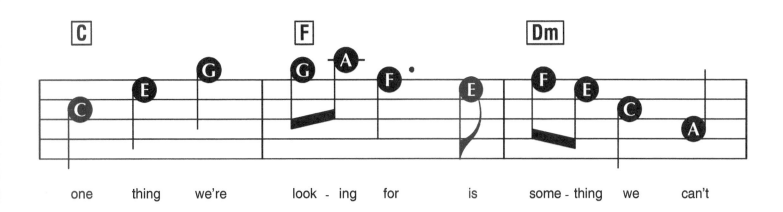

one   thing   we're   look - ing   for   is   some - thing   we   can't

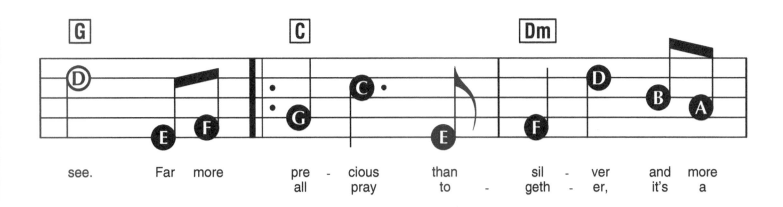

see.   Far   more   pre - cious   than   sil - ver   and   more
                    all   pray   to - geth - er,   it's   a

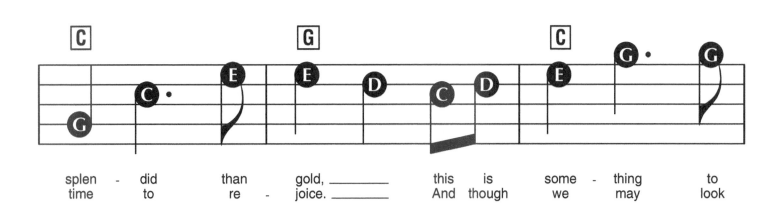

splen - did   than   gold, _____   this   is   some - thing   to
time   to   re - joice. _____   And though   we   may   look

12

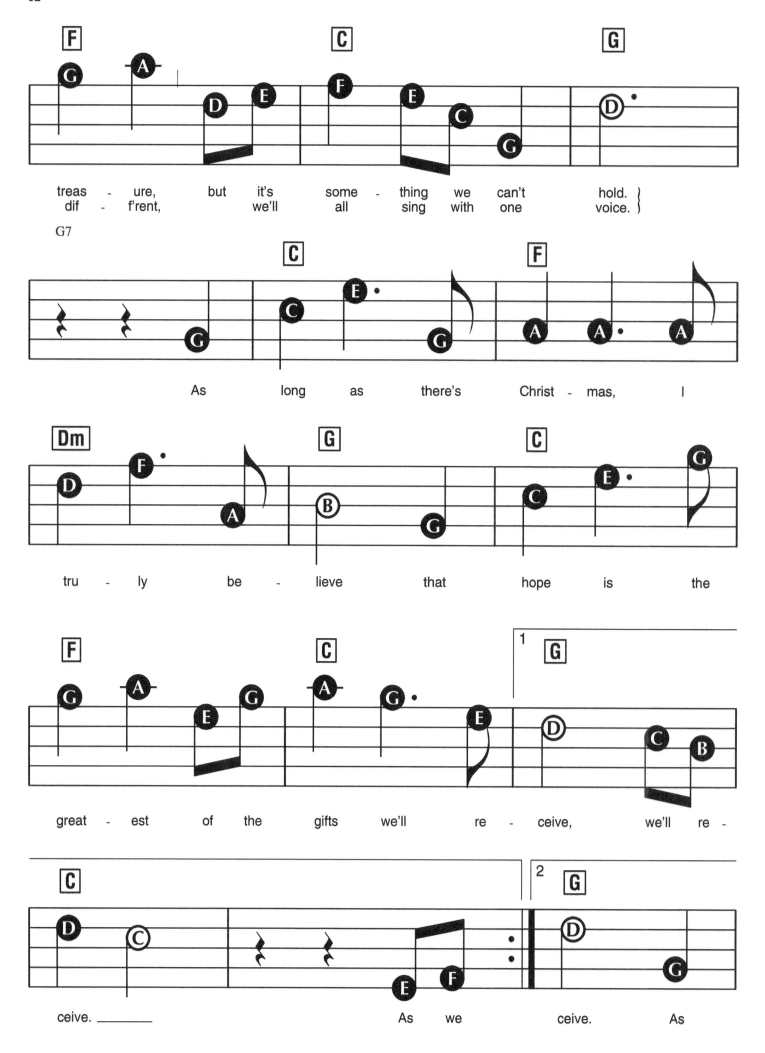

13

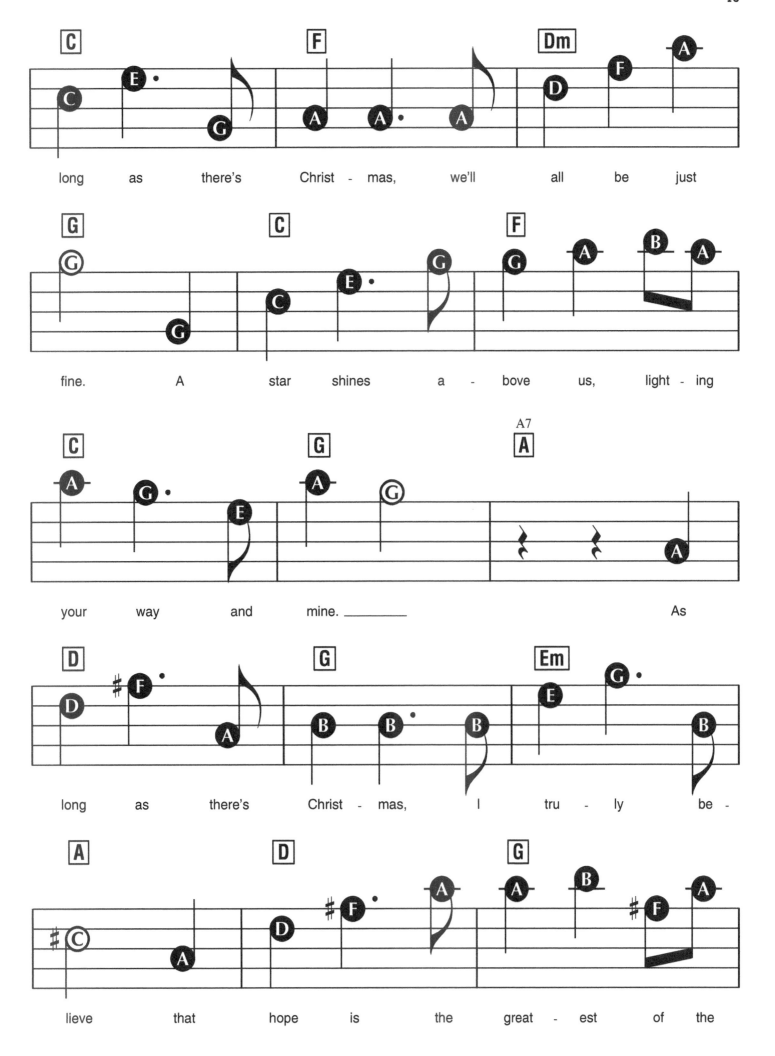

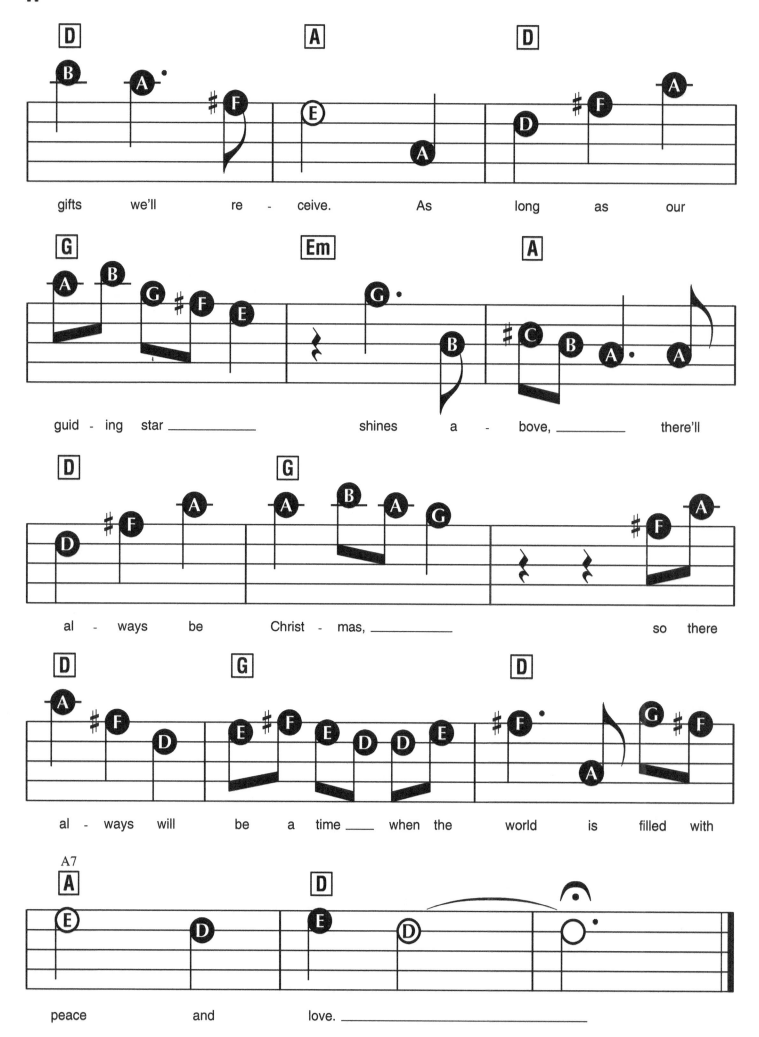

Because It's Christmas
(For All the Children)

Registration 2
Rhythm: Swing

Music by Barry Manilow
Lyric by Bruce Sussman and Jack Feldman

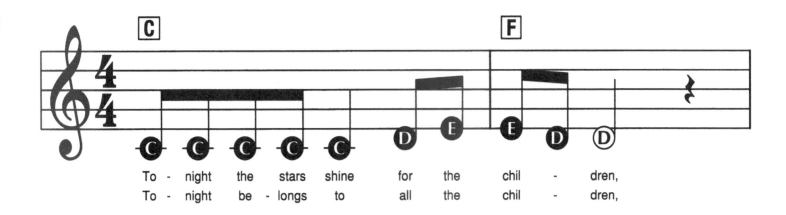

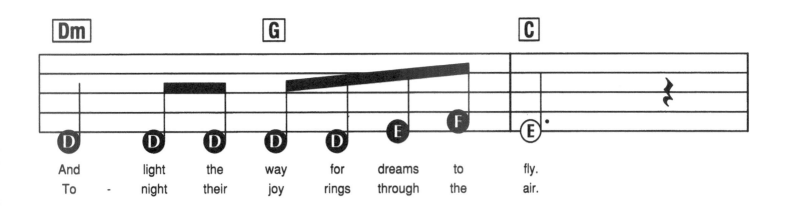

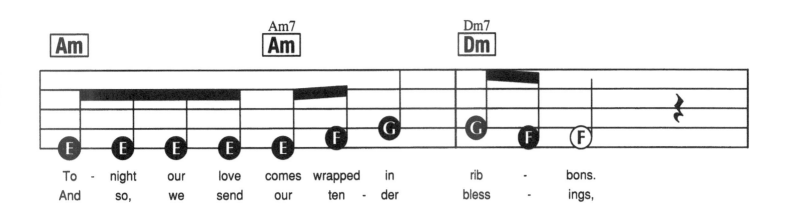

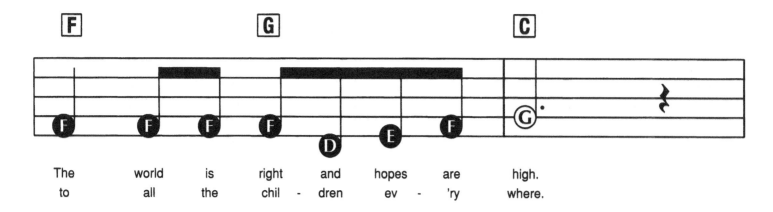

The world is right and hopes are high.
to all the chil - dren ev - 'ry where.

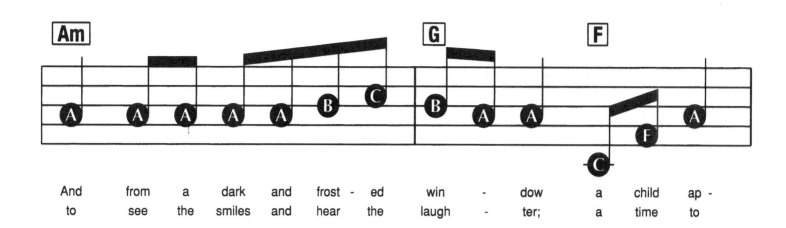

And from a dark and frost - ed win - dow a child ap -
to see the smiles and hear the laugh - ter; a time to

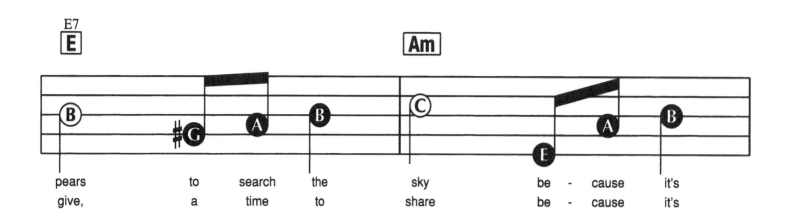

pears to search the sky be - cause it's
give, a time to share be - cause it's

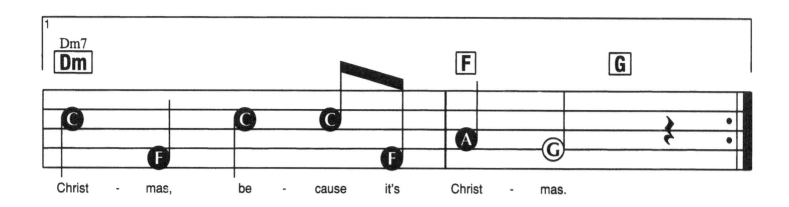

Christ - mas, be - cause it's Christ - mas.

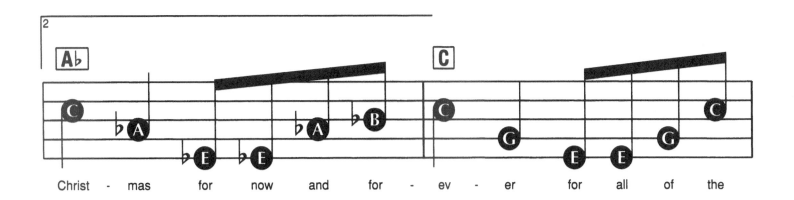

Christ - mas for now and for - ev - er for all of the

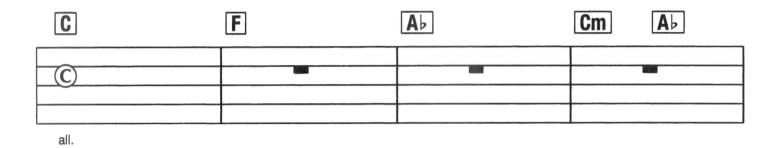

chil - dren and for the chil - dren in us

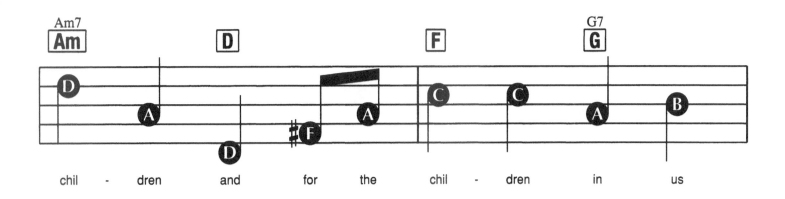

all.

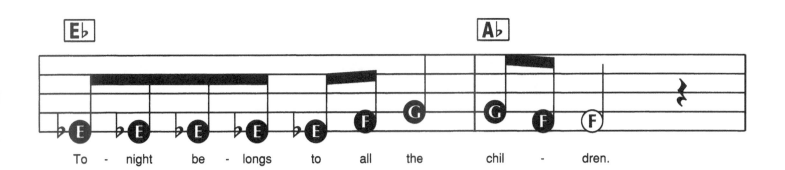

To - night be - longs to all the chil - dren.

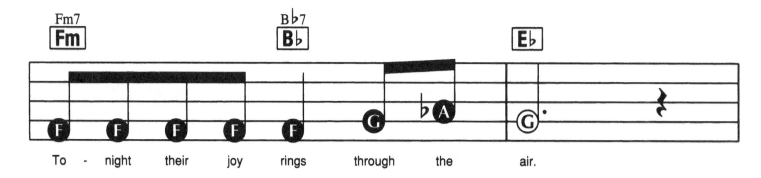

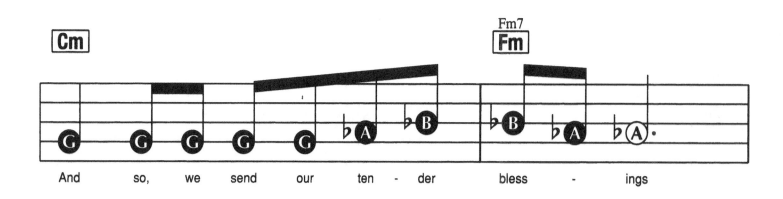

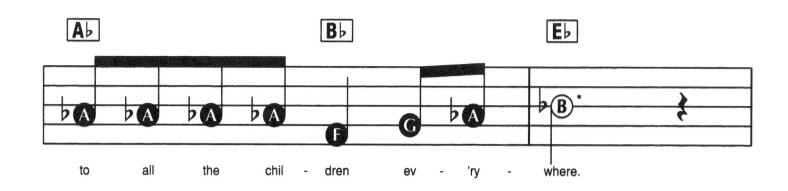

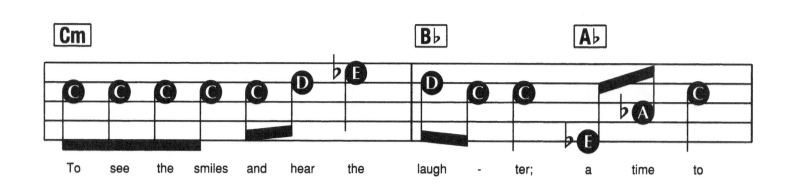

19

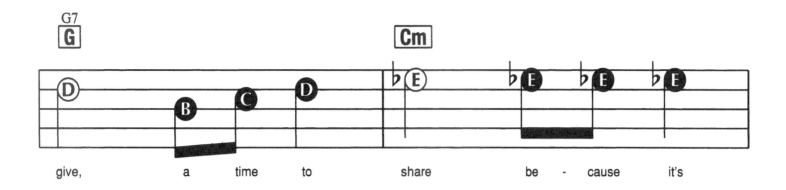

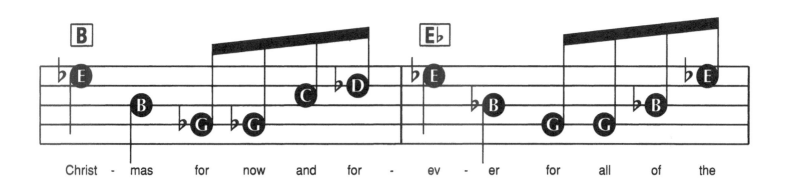

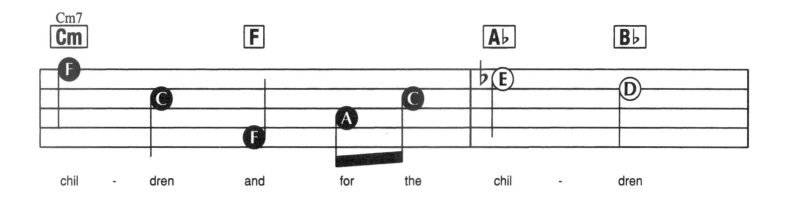

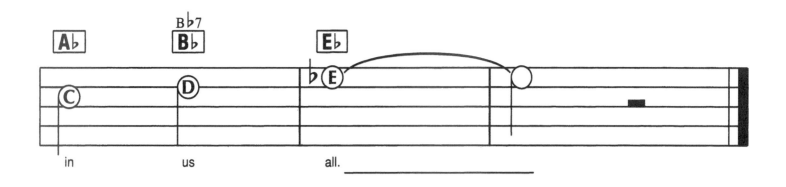

Blue Christmas

Registration 3
Rhythm: Fox Trot or Swing

Words and Music by Billy Hayes
and Jay Johnson

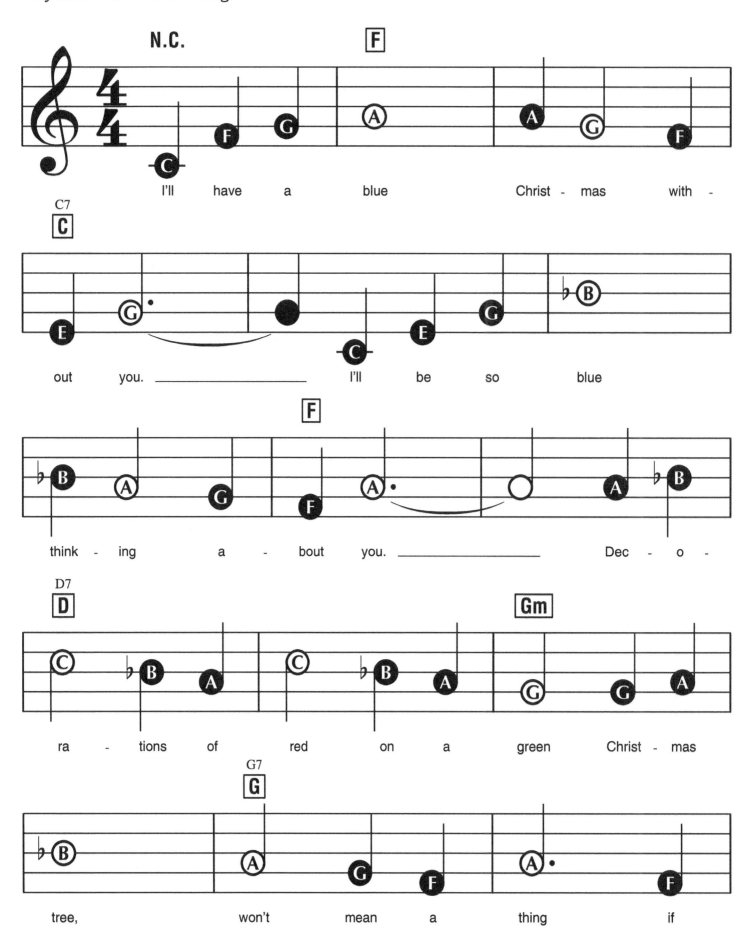

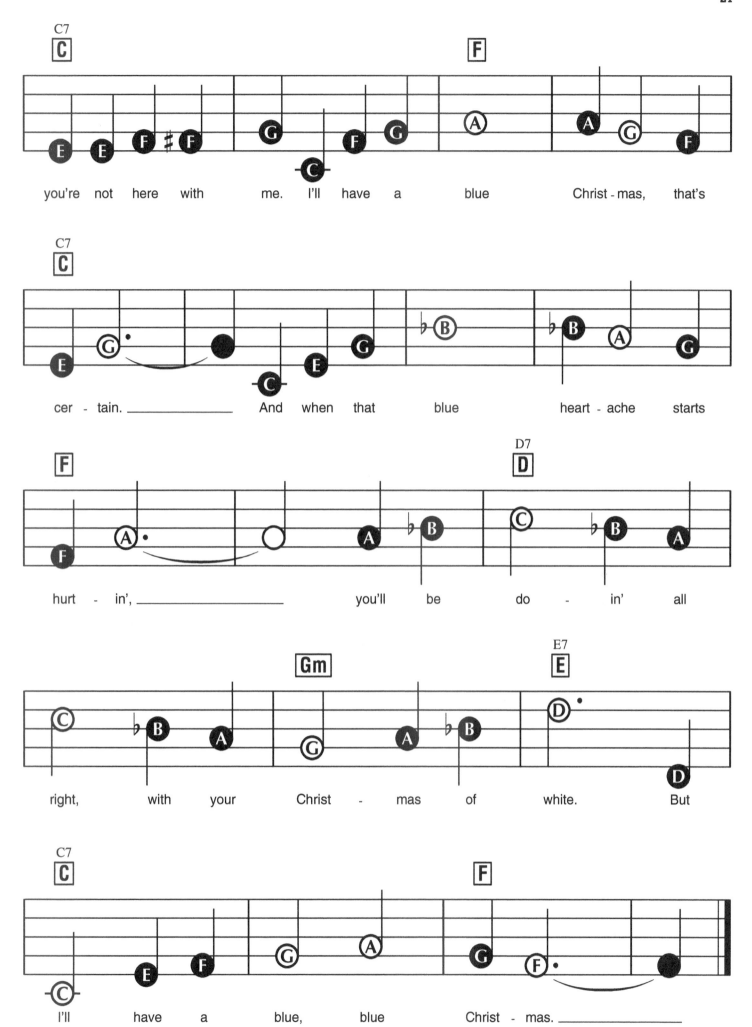

Christmas Is

Registration 10
Rhythm: Fox Trot or Slow Swing

Lyrics by Spence Maxwell
Music by Percy Faith

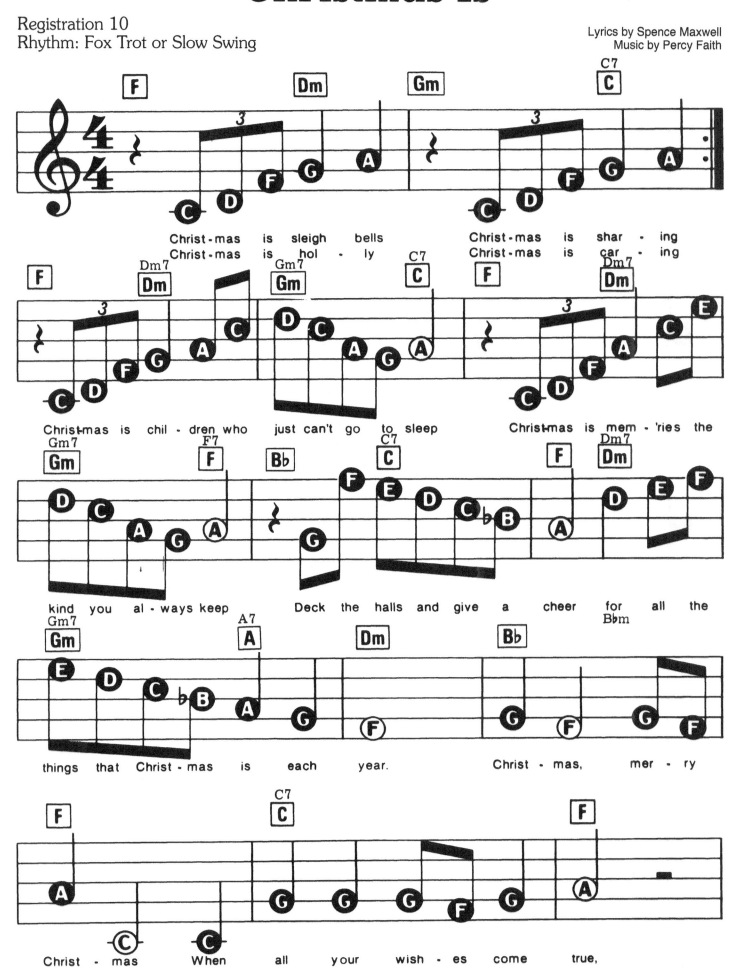

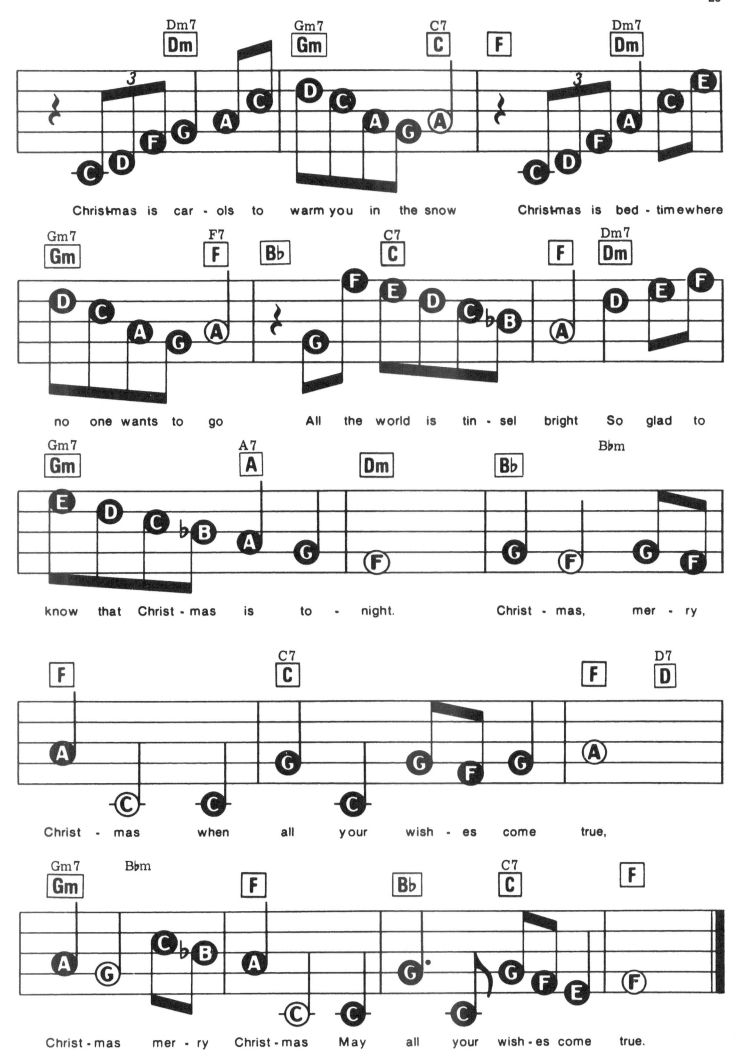

Christmas in Dixie

Registration 2
Rhythm: 8 Beat or Rock

Words and Music by Jeffrey Cook,
Teddy Gentry, Mark Herndon
and Randy Owen

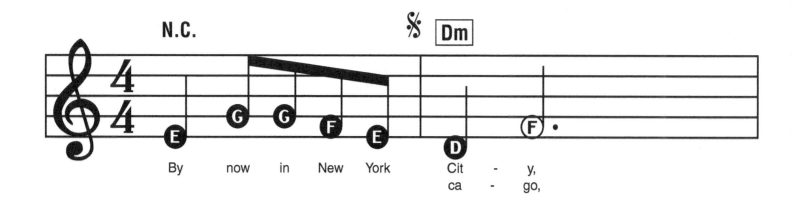

By now in New York Cit - y,
ca - go,

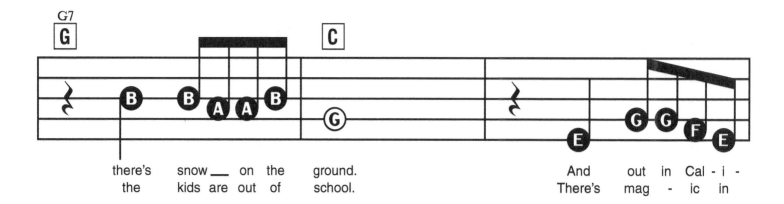

there's snow ___ on the ground.
the kids are out of school.

And out in Cal - i -
There's mag - ic in

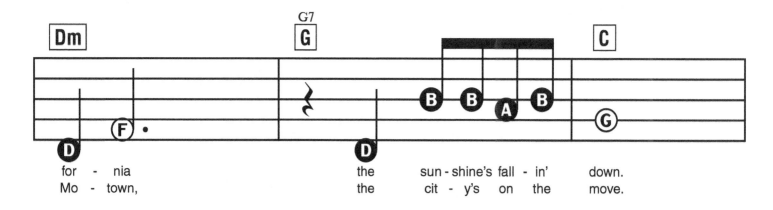

for - nia the sun - shine's fall - in' down.
Mo - town, the cit - y's on the move.

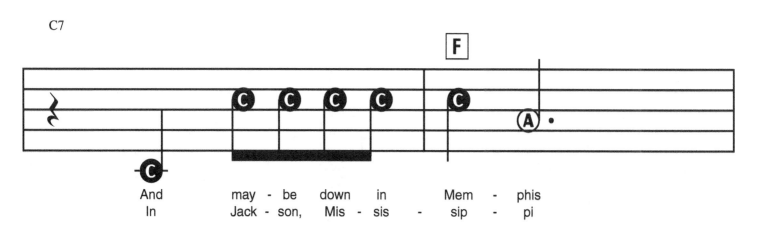

And may - be down in Mem - phis
In Jack - son, Mis - sis - sip - pi

D.S. al Coda
(Return to %
Play to ⊕ and
Skip to Coda)

It's wind - y in Chi -

CODA
⊕

And from Fort Payne, Al - a - ba - ma,

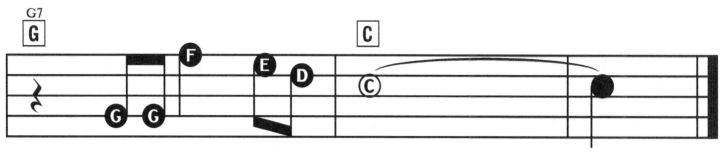

mer - ry Christ - mas to - night. _____

Christmas Is A-Comin'
(May God Bless You)

Registration 1
Rhythm: Ballad

Words and Music by
Frank Luther

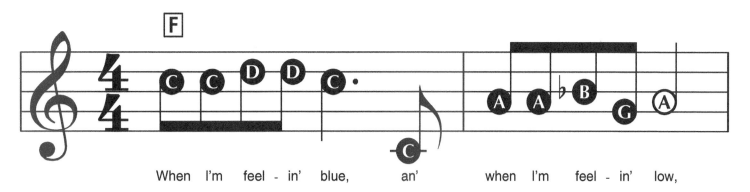

When I'm feel - in' blue, an' when I'm feel - in' low,

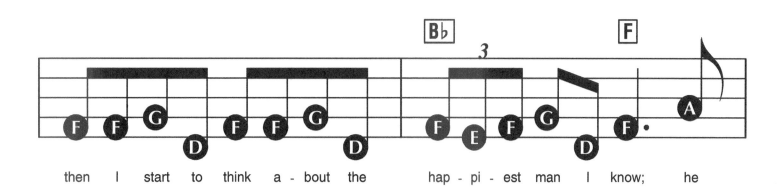

then I start to think a - bout the hap - pi - est man I know; he

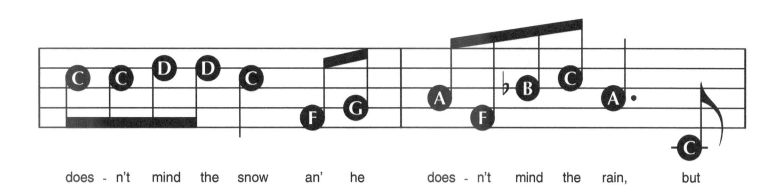

does - n't mind the snow an' he does - n't mind the rain, but

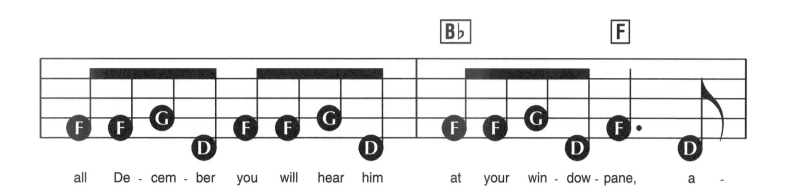

all De - cem - ber you will hear him at your win - dow - pane, a -

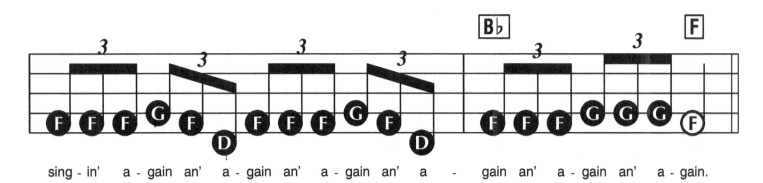

sing - in' a - gain an' a - gain an' a - gain an' a - gain an' a - gain an' a - gain.

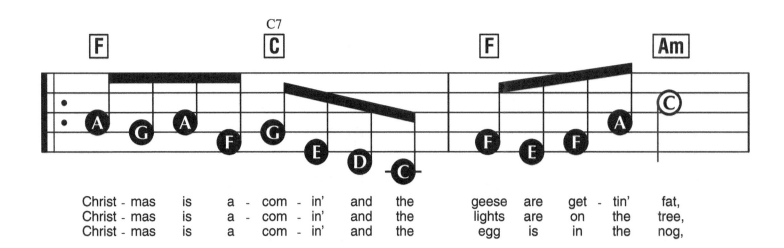

Christ - mas is a - com - in' and the geese are get - tin' fat,
Christ - mas is a - com - in' and the lights are on the tree,
Christ - mas is a - com - in' and the egg is in the nog,

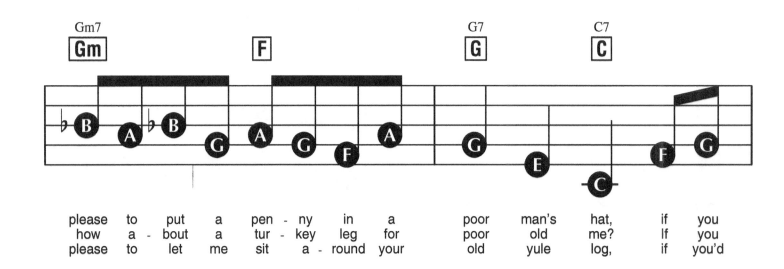

please to put a pen - ny in a poor man's hat, if you
how a - bout a tur - key leg for poor old me? If you
please to let me sit a - round your old yule log, if you'd

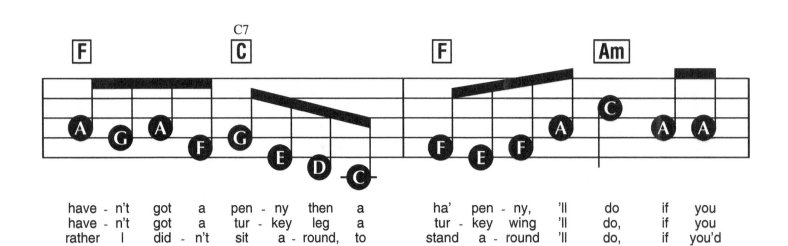

have - n't got a pen - ny then a ha' pen - ny, 'll do if you
have - n't got a tur - key leg a tur - key wing 'll do, if you
rather I did - n't sit a - round, to stand a - round 'll do, if you'd

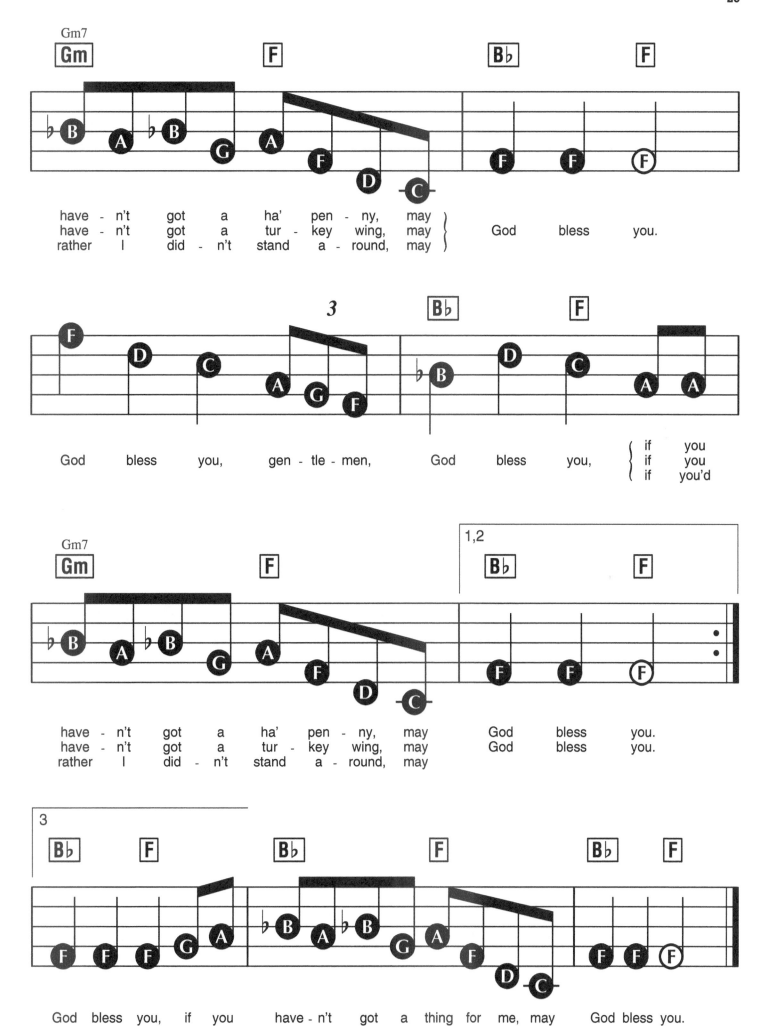

The Christmas Song
(Chestnuts Roasting on an Open Fire)

Registration 2
Rhythm: Ballad or Fox Trot

Music and Lyric by Mel Torme
and Robert Wells

Chest-nuts roast-ing on an op-en fire, Jack Frost nip-ping at your

nose, Yule-tide car-ols be-ing sung by a choir And

folks dressed up like Es-ki-mos. Ev-'ry-bod-y knows a tur-key and some

mis-tle-toe Help to make the sea-son bright. Ti-ny tots with their

eyes all a-glow Will find it hard to sleep to-night. They know that

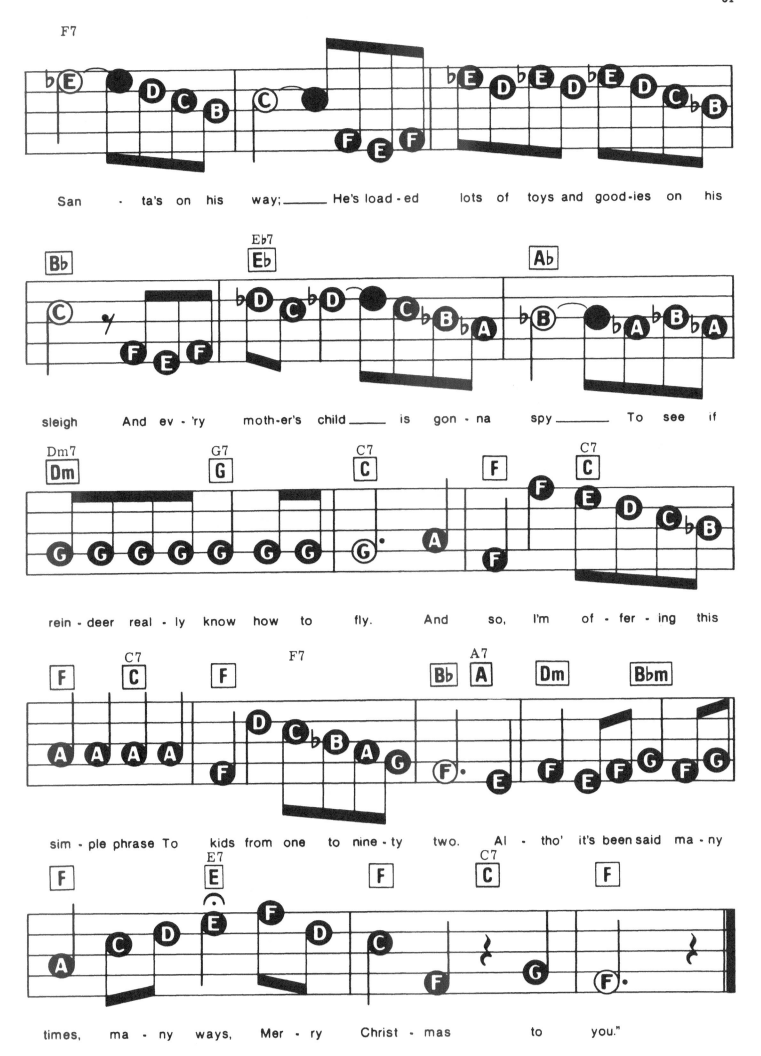

Christmas Time Is Here
from A CHARLIE BROWN CHRISTMAS

Registration 8
Rhythm: Waltz

Words by Lee Mendelson
Music by Vince Guaraldi

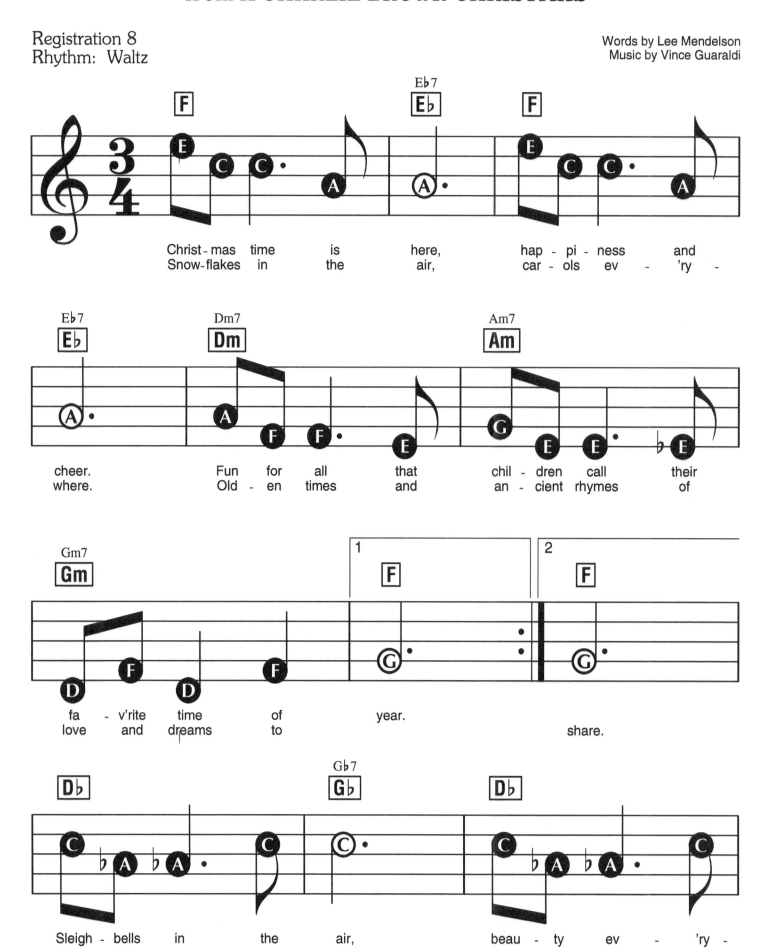

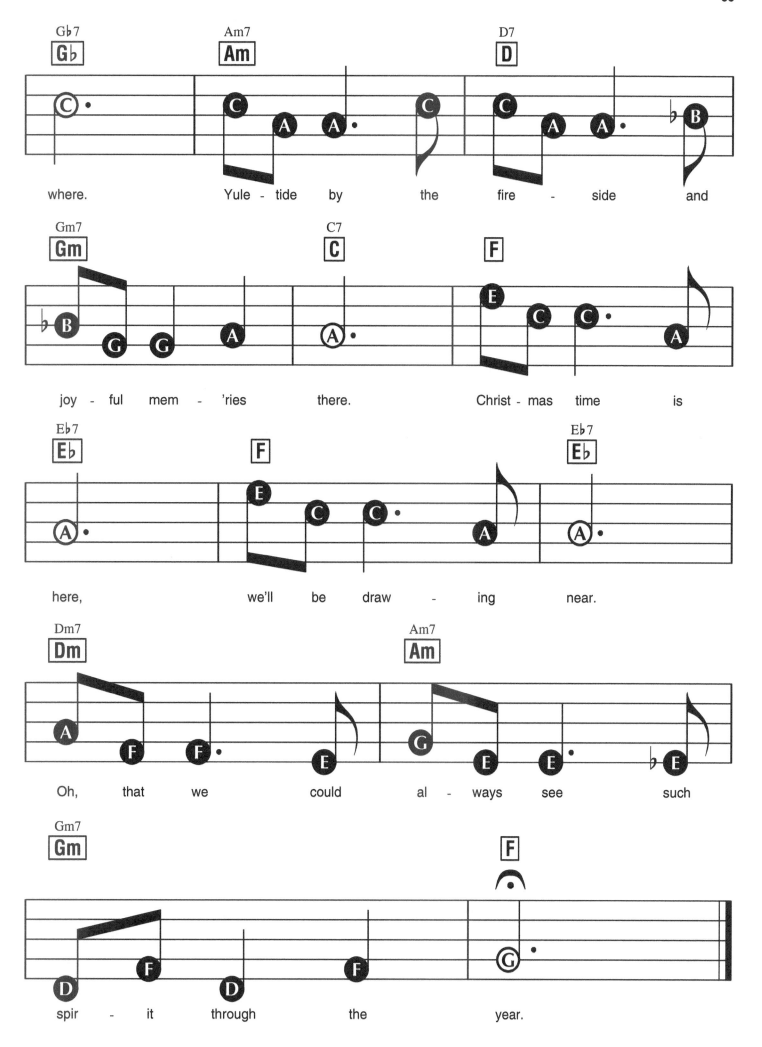

White Christmas
from the Motion Picture Irving Berlin's HOLIDAY INN

Registration 10
Rhythm: Rock or Pops

Words and Music by
Irving Berlin

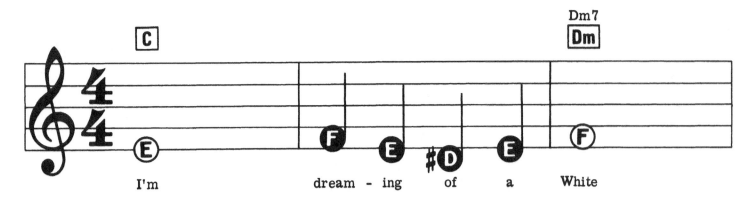

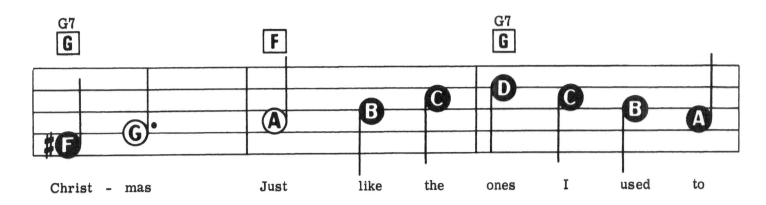

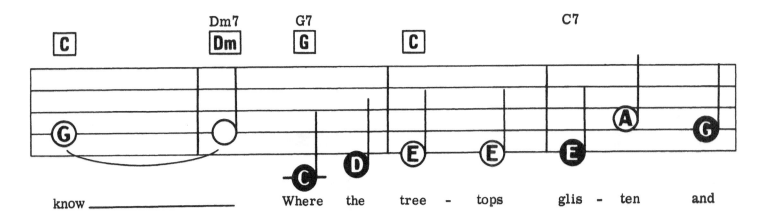

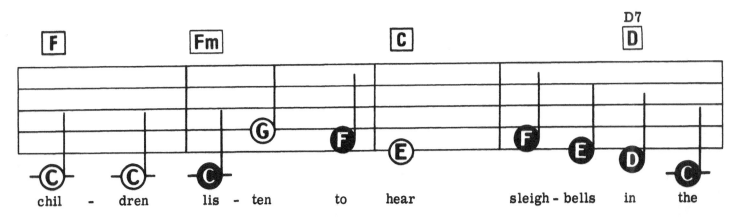

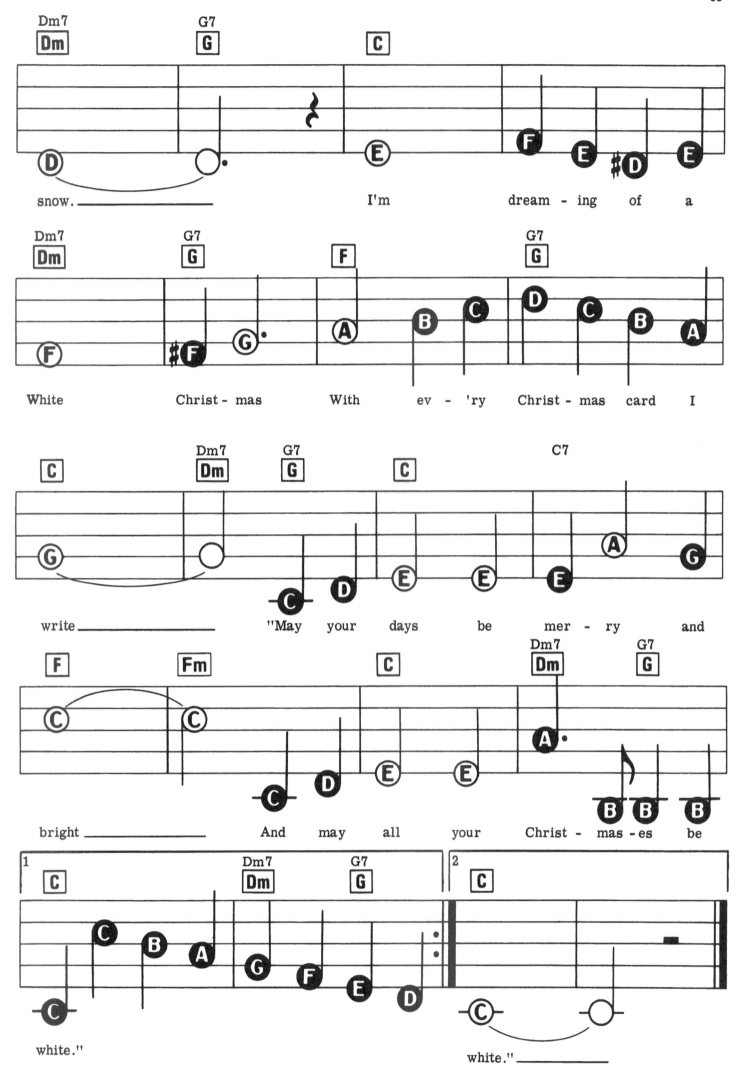

The Christmas Waltz

Words by Sammy Cahn
Music by Jule Styne

Registration 2
Rhythm: Waltz

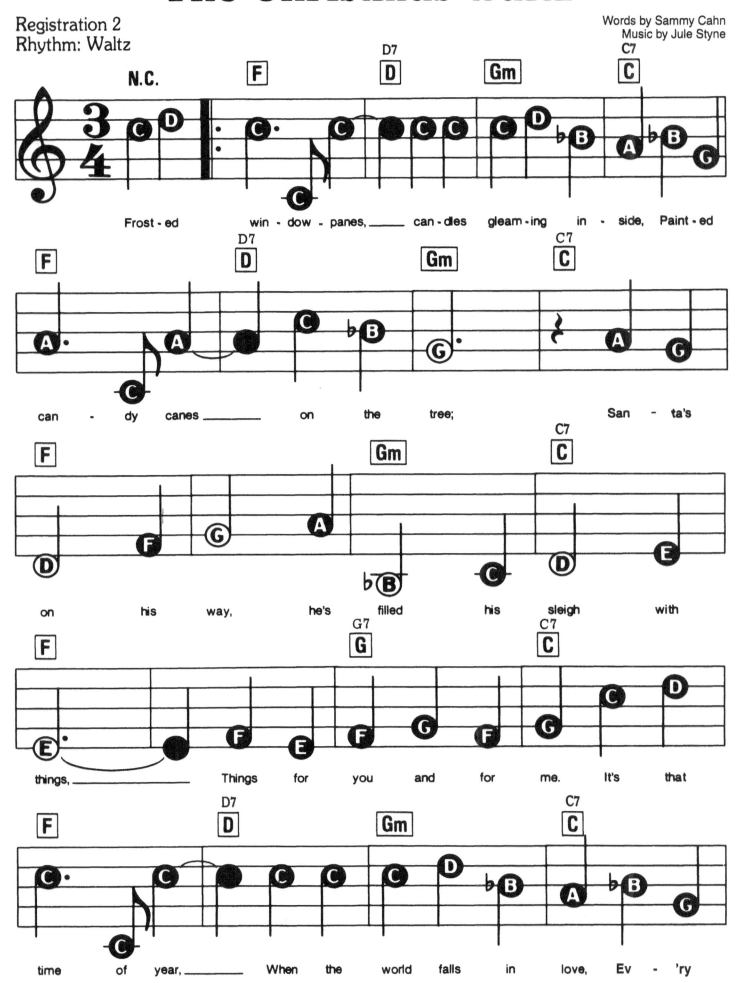

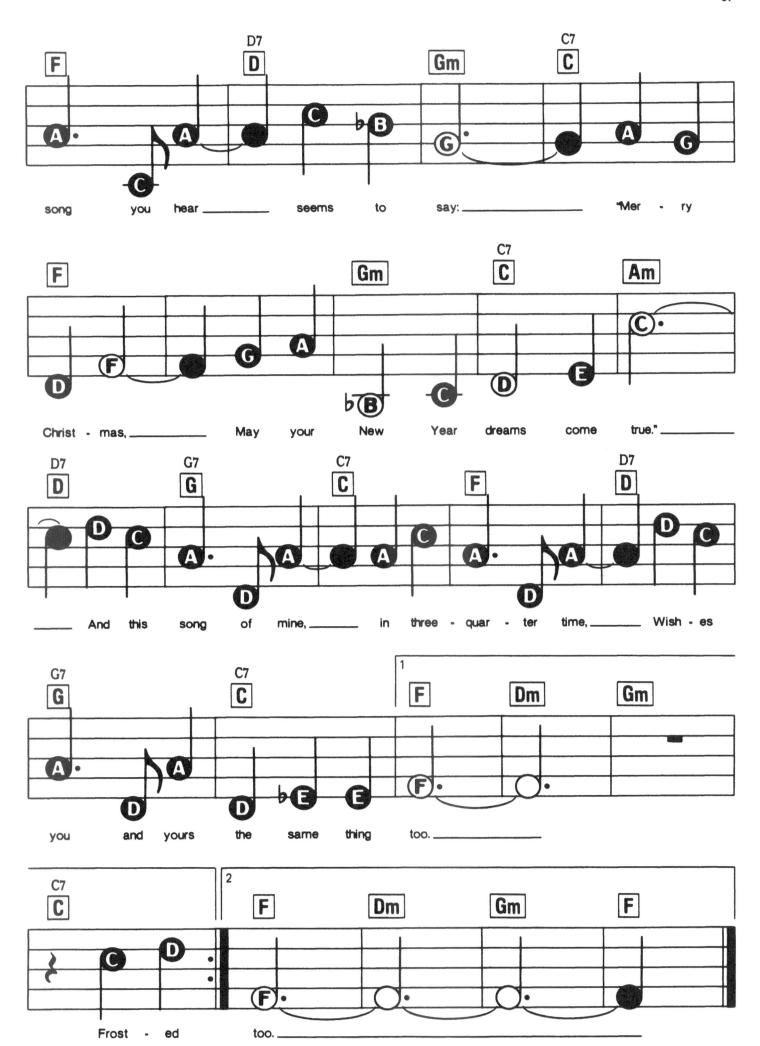

Deck the Hall

Registration 5
Rhythm: Fox Trot

Traditional Welsh Carol

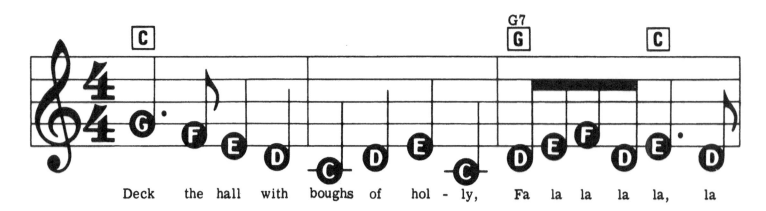

Deck the hall with boughs of hol - ly, Fa la la la la, la

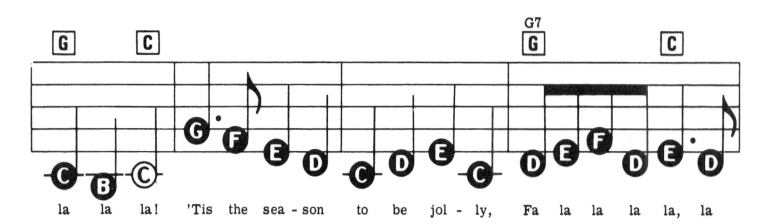

la la la! 'Tis the sea - son to be jol - ly, Fa la la la la, la

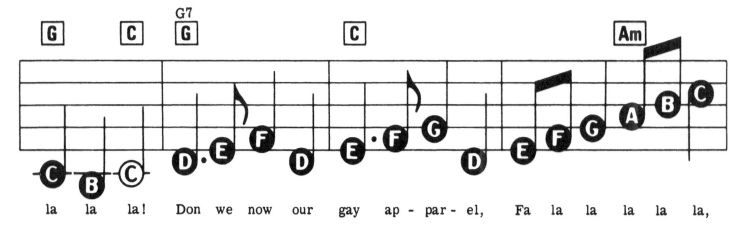

la la la! Don we now our gay ap - par - el, Fa la la la la la,

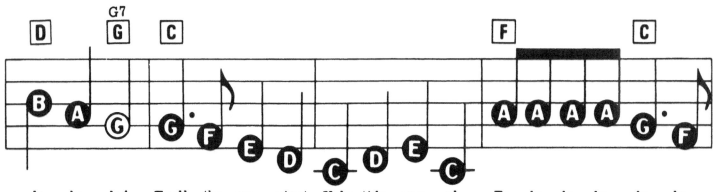

la la la! Troll the an - cient Yule - tide car - ol, Fa la la la la, la

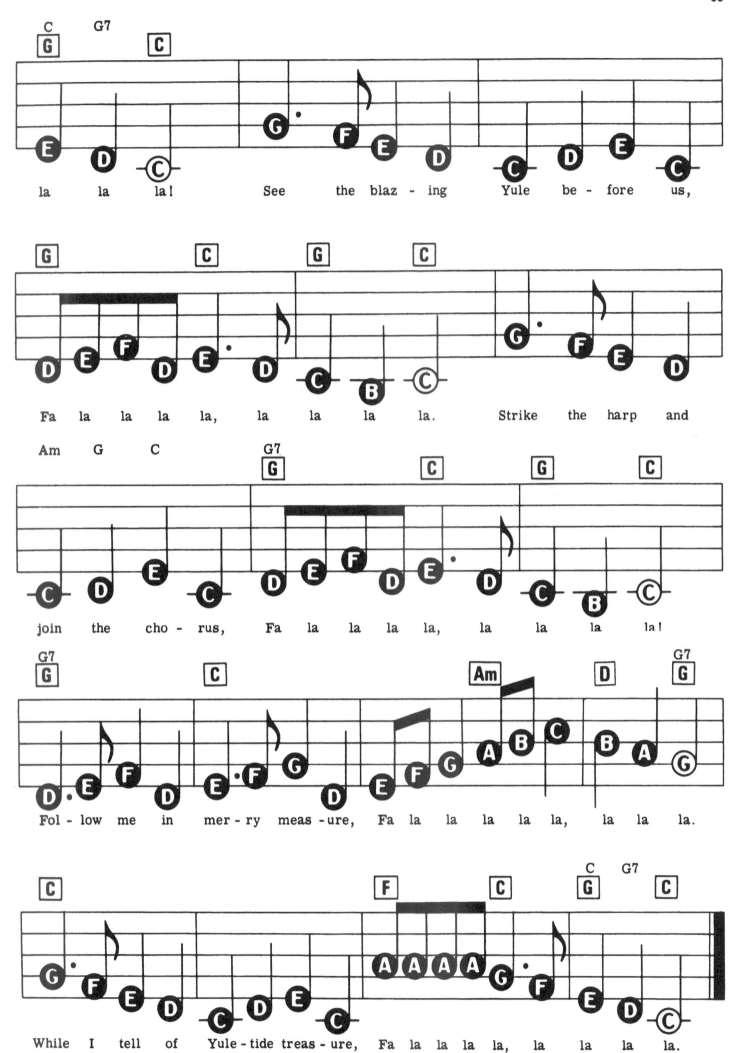

Feliz Navidad

Registration 1
Rhythm: Latin or Bossa Nova

Music and Lyrics by
José Feliciano

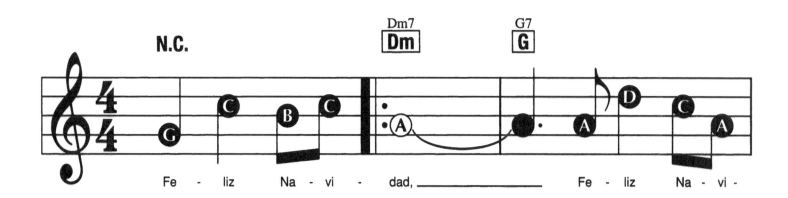

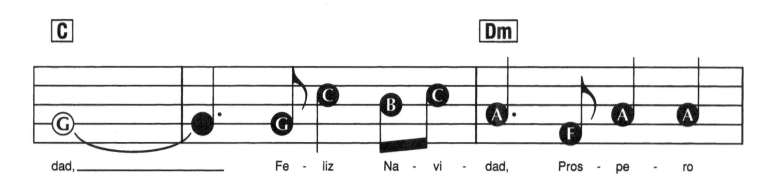

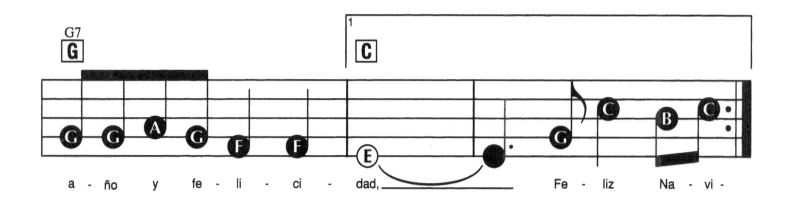

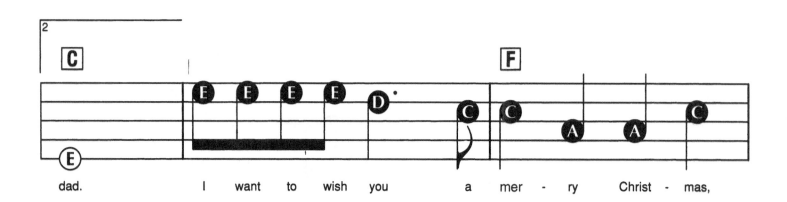

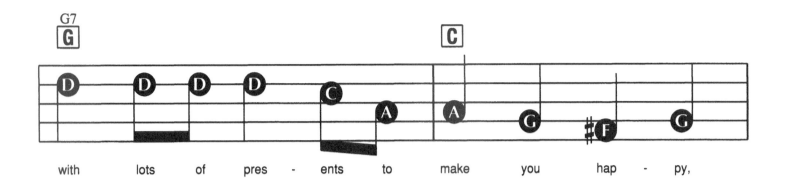

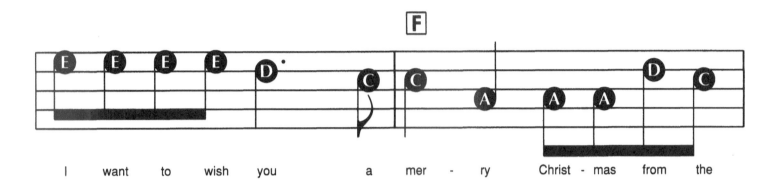

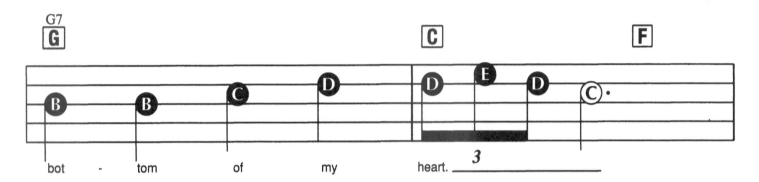

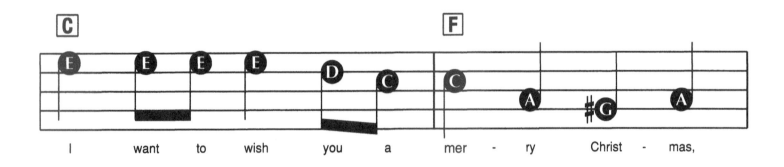

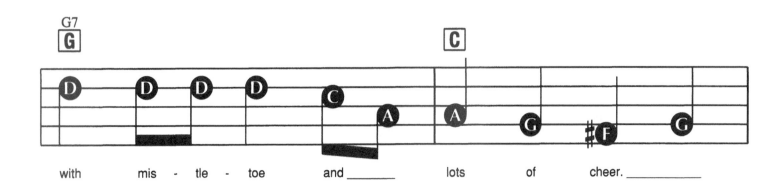

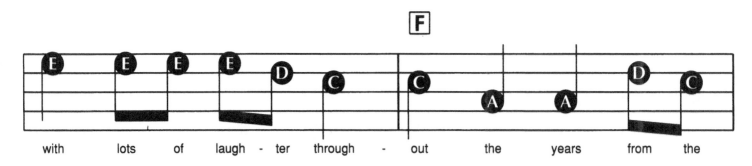

with lots of laugh - ter through - out the years from the

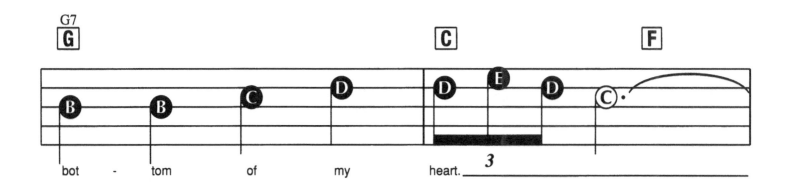

bot - tom of my heart. _____ 3 _____

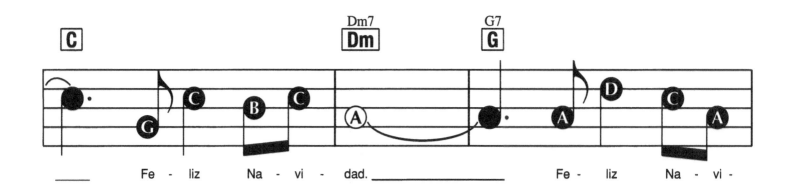

_____ Fe - liz Na - vi - dad. _____ Fe - liz Na - vi -

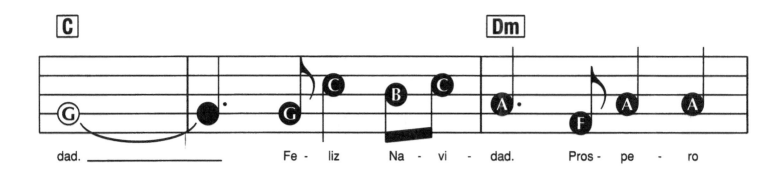

dad. _____ Fe - liz Na - vi - dad. Pros - pe - ro

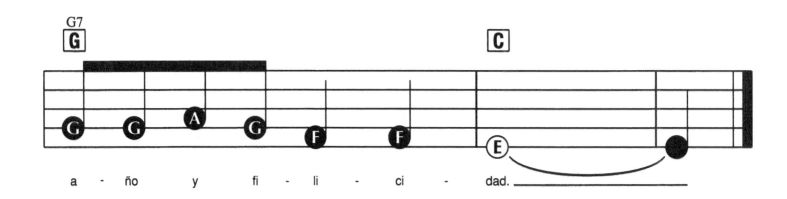

a - ño y fi - li - ci - dad. _____

The Gift

Registration 9
Rhythm: Ballad

Words and Music by Tom Douglas
and Jim Brickman

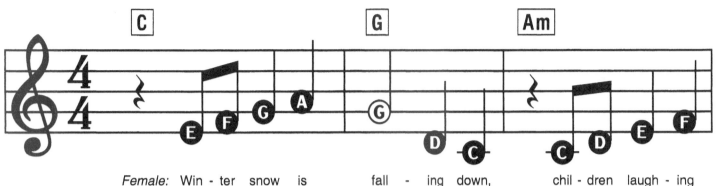

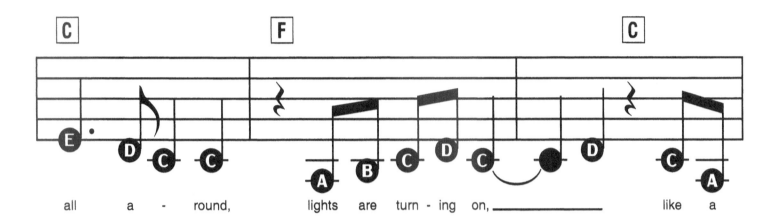

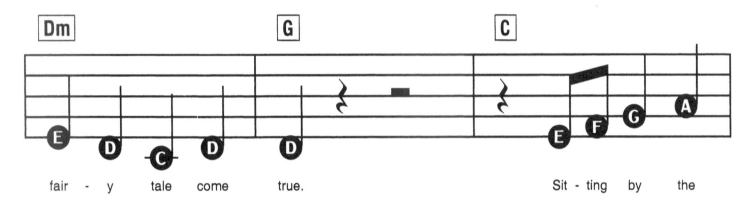

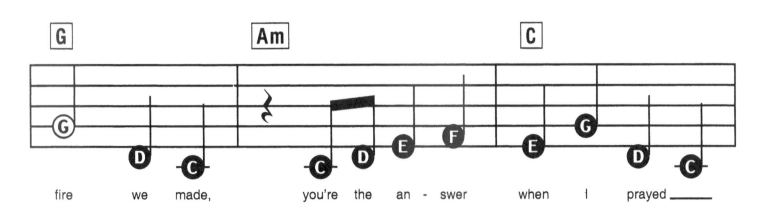

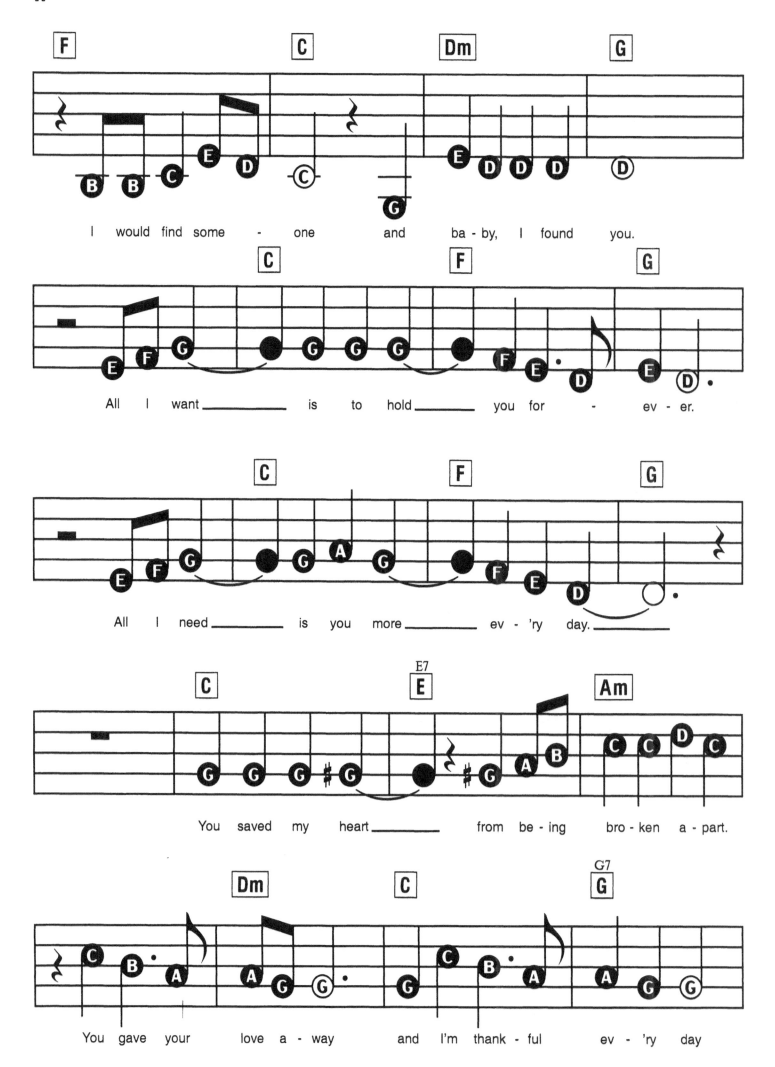

45

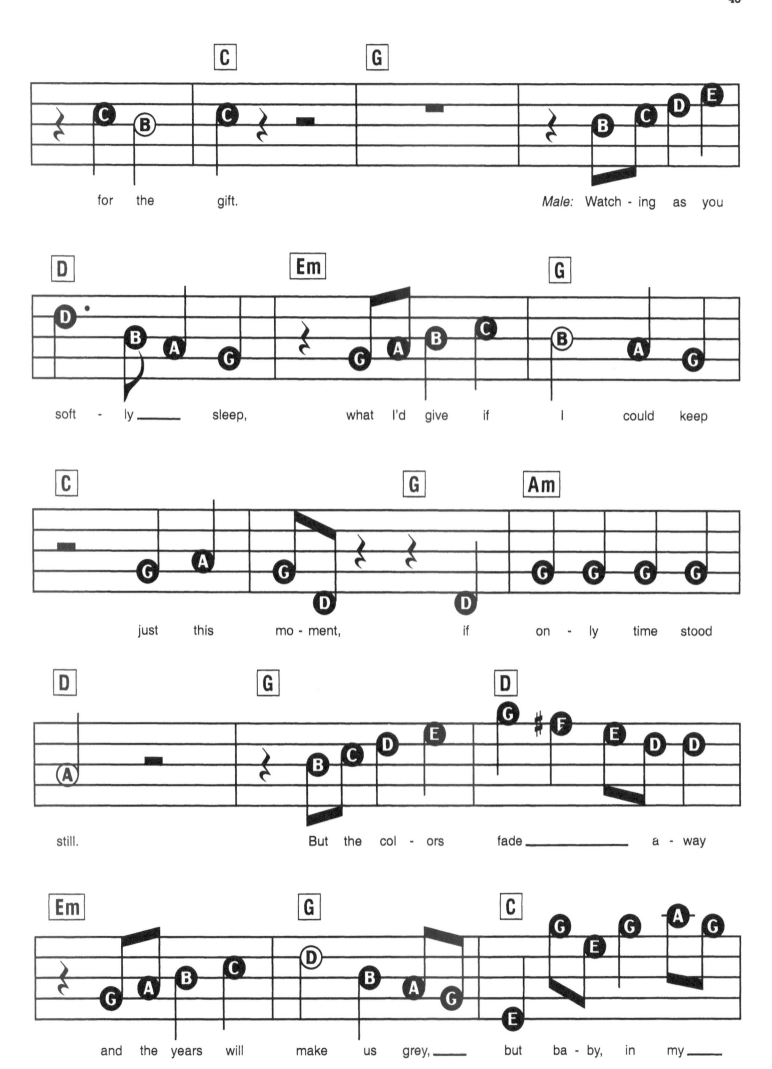

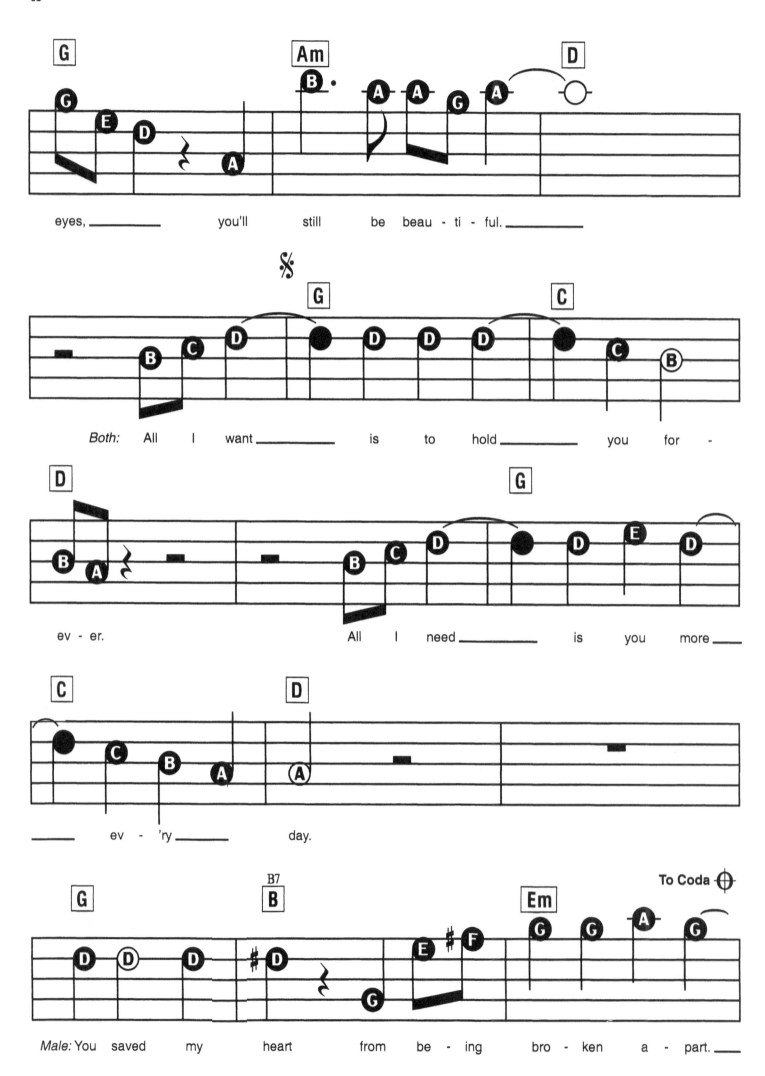

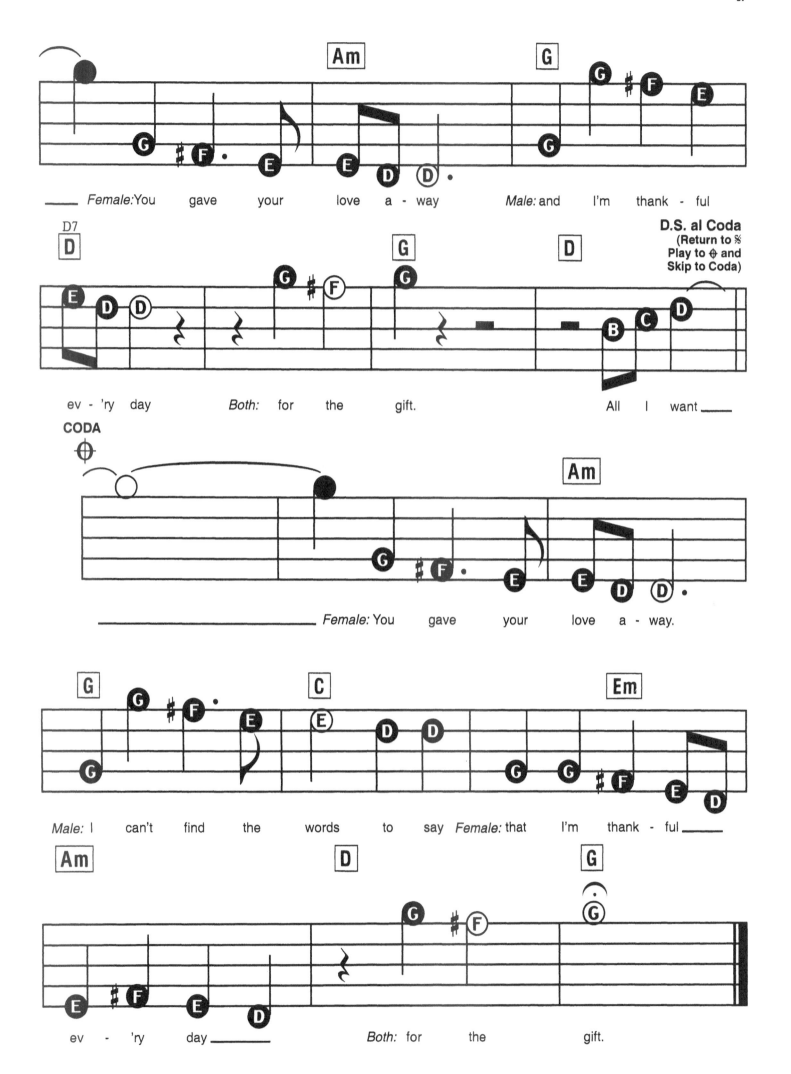

The First Chanukah Night

Registration 3
Rhythm: Fox Trot

Words by Enid Futterman
Music by Michael Cohen

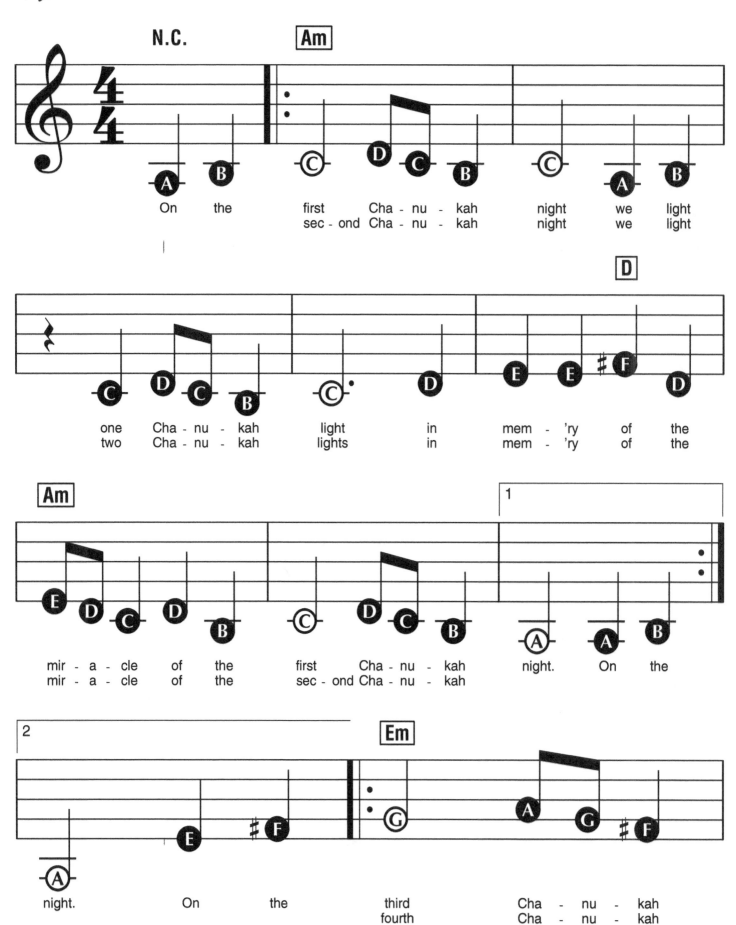

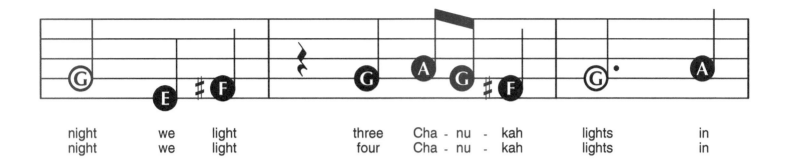

night we light three Cha - nu - kah lights in
night we light four Cha - nu - kah lights in

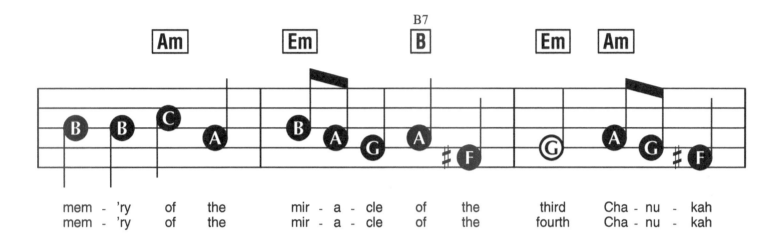

mem - 'ry of the mir - a - cle of the third Cha - nu - kah
mem - 'ry of the mir - a - cle of the fourth Cha - nu - kah

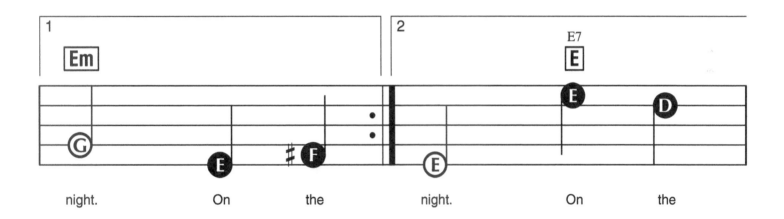

night. On the night. On the

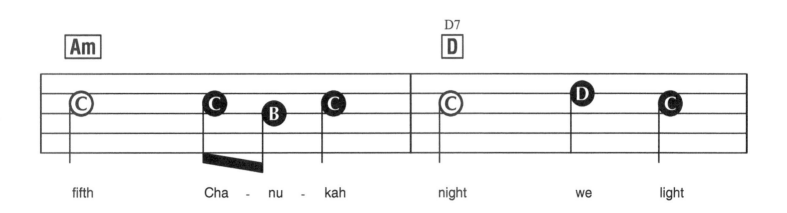

fifth Cha - nu - kah night we light

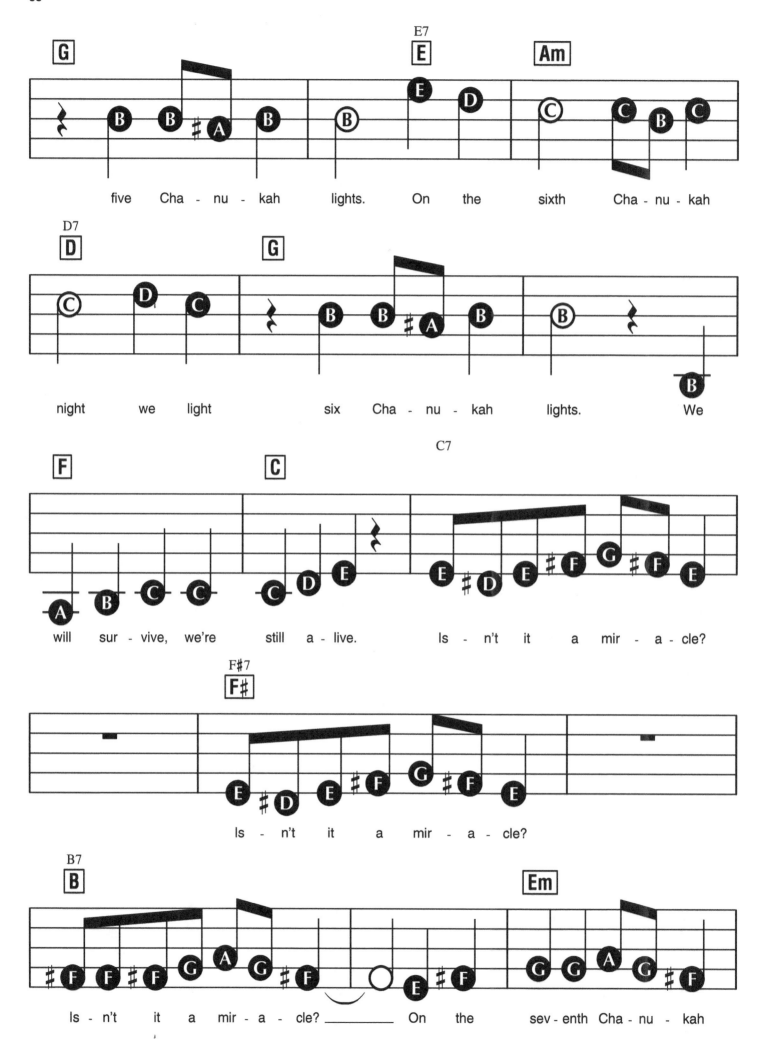

51

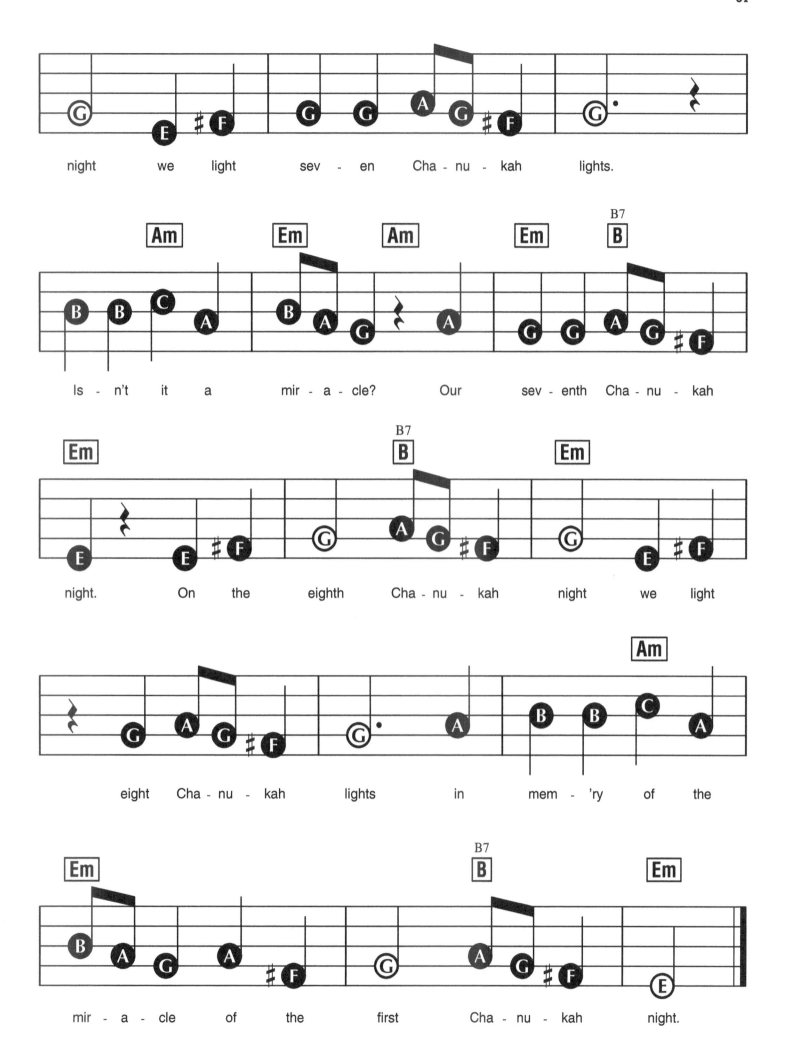

God Rest Ye Merry, Gentlemen

Registration 6
Rhythm: None

19th Century English Carol

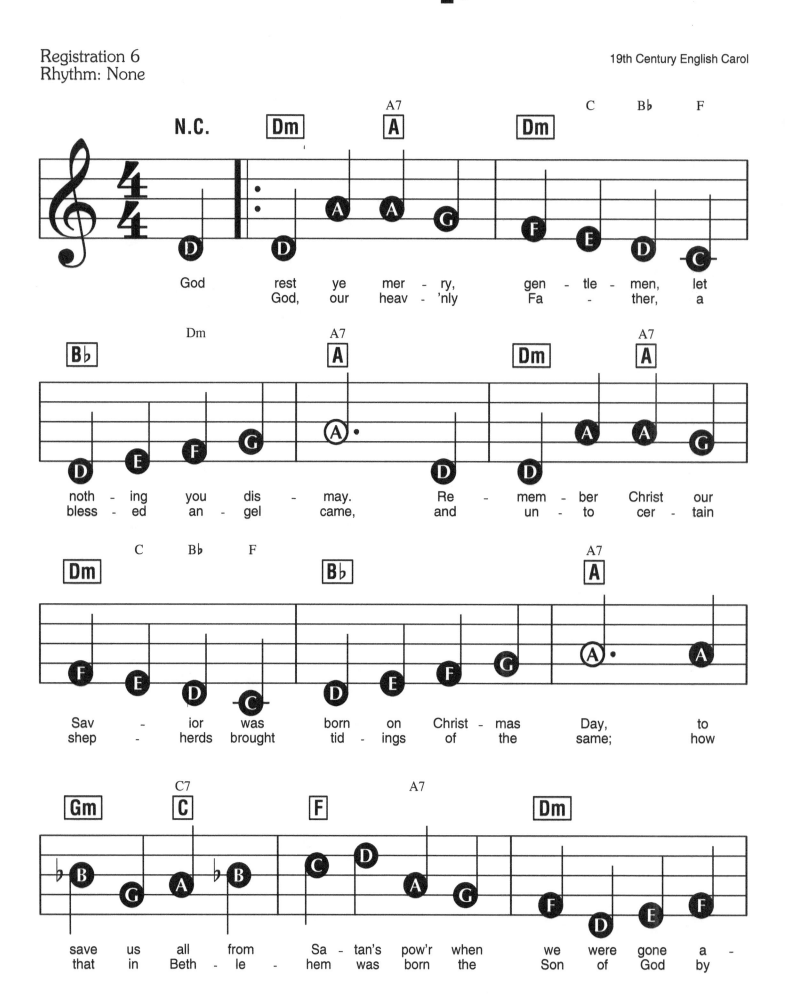

53

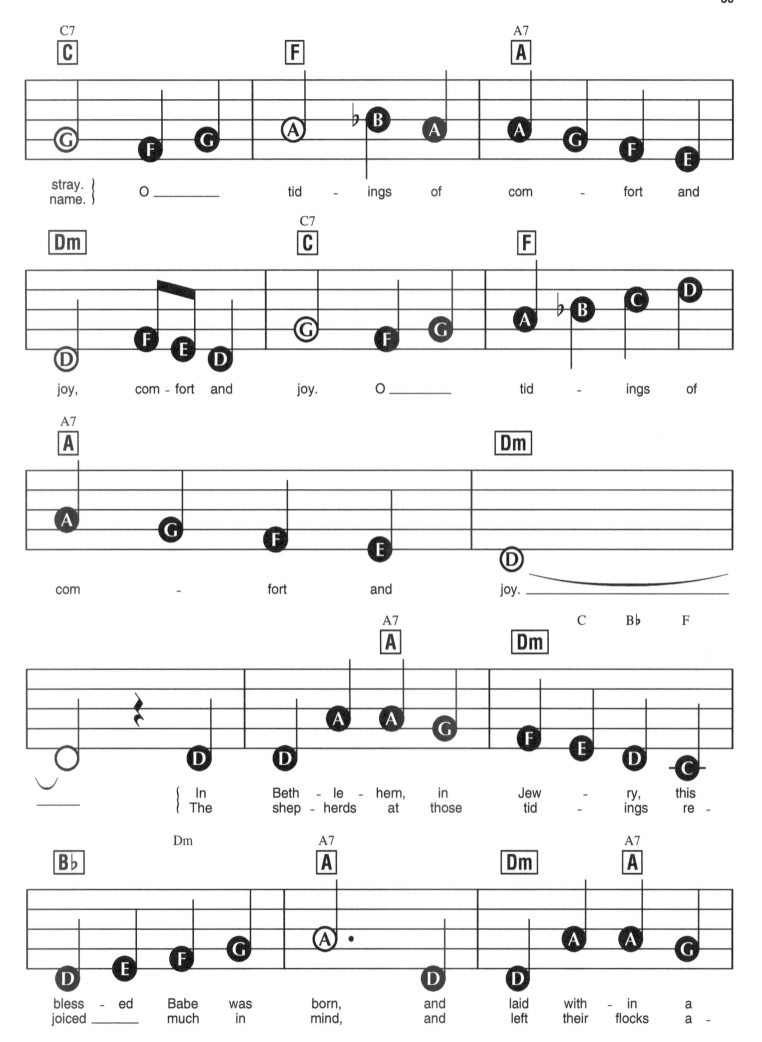

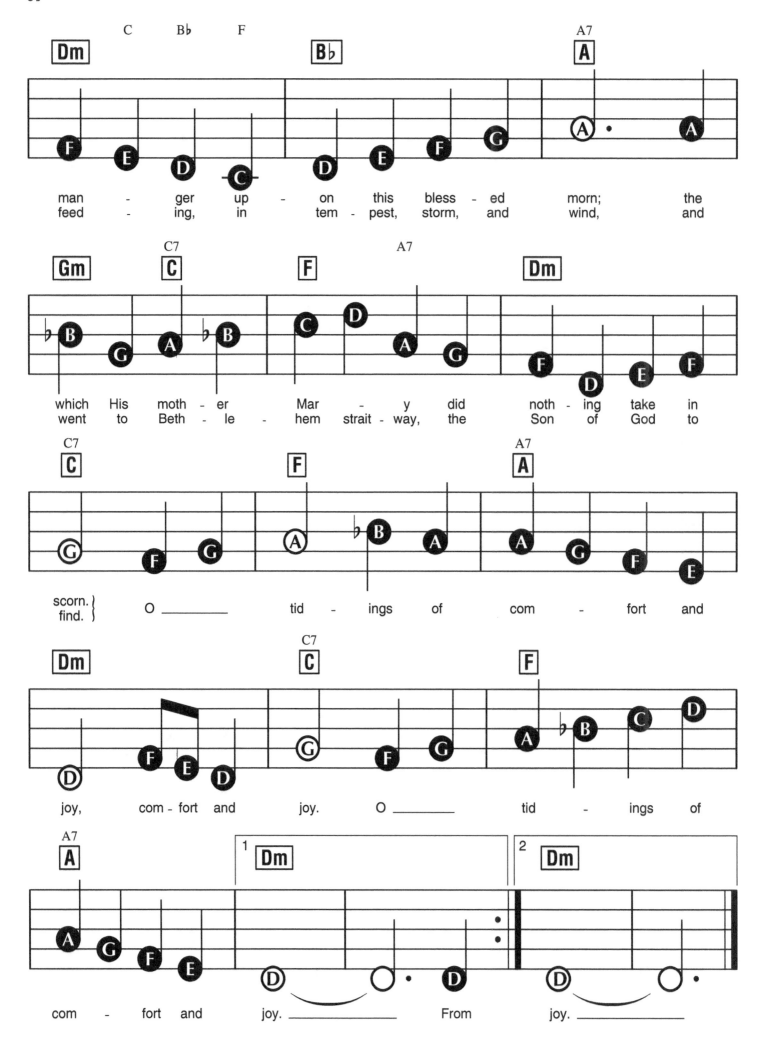

Grandma Got Run Over by a Reindeer

Registration 2
Rhythm: Fox Trot or Swing

Words and Music by
Randy Brooks

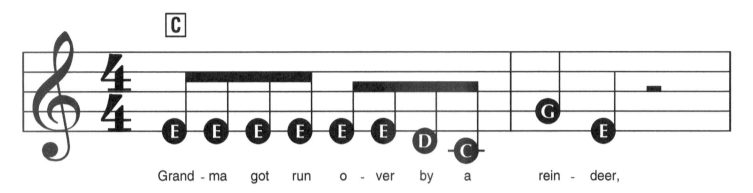

Grand - ma got run o - ver by a rein - deer,

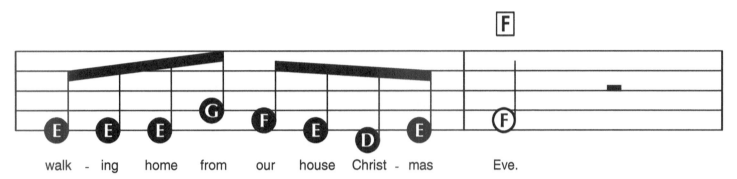

walk - ing home from our house Christ - mas Eve.

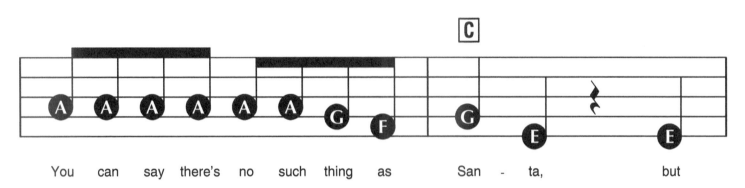

You can say there's no such thing as San - ta, but

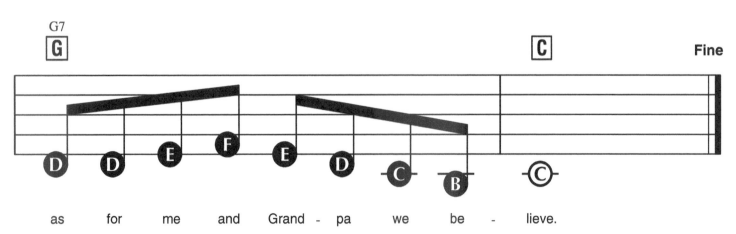

as for me and Grand - pa we be - lieve.

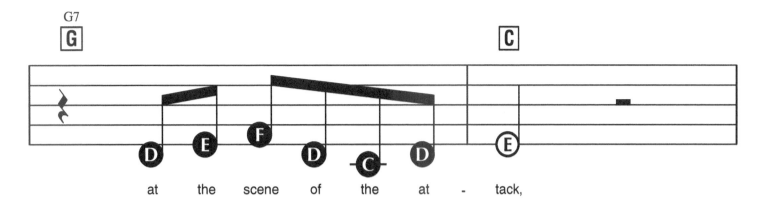

at the scene of the at - tack,

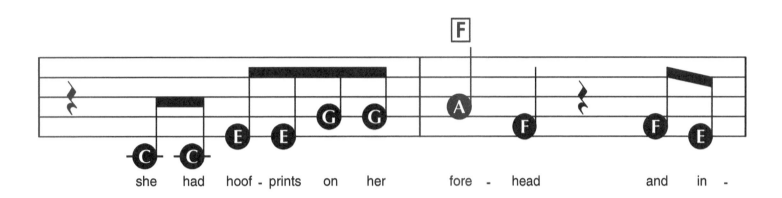

she had hoof - prints on her fore - head and in -

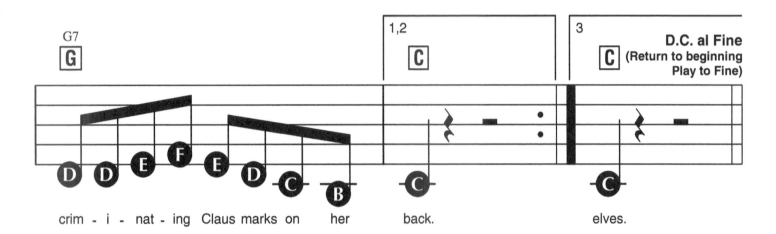

crim - i - nat - ing Claus marks on her back. elves.

D.C. al Fine
(Return to beginning Play to Fine)

Additional Lyrics

2. Now we're all so proud of Grandpa,
He's been taking this so well.
See him in there watching football,
Drinking beer and playing cards with Cousin Mel.
It's not Christmas without Grandma,
All the family's dressed in black,
And we just can't help but wonder:
Should we open up her gifts or send them back? *(To Chorus:)*

3. Now the goose is on the table
And the pudding made of fig.
And the blue and silver candles,
That would just have matched the hair in Grandma's wig.
I've warned all my friends and neighbors,
Better watch out for yourselves.
They should never give a license,
To a man who drives a sleigh and plays with elves. *(To Chorus:)*

The Greatest Gift of All

Registration 4
Rhythm: Shuffle or Country

Words and Music by
John Jarvis

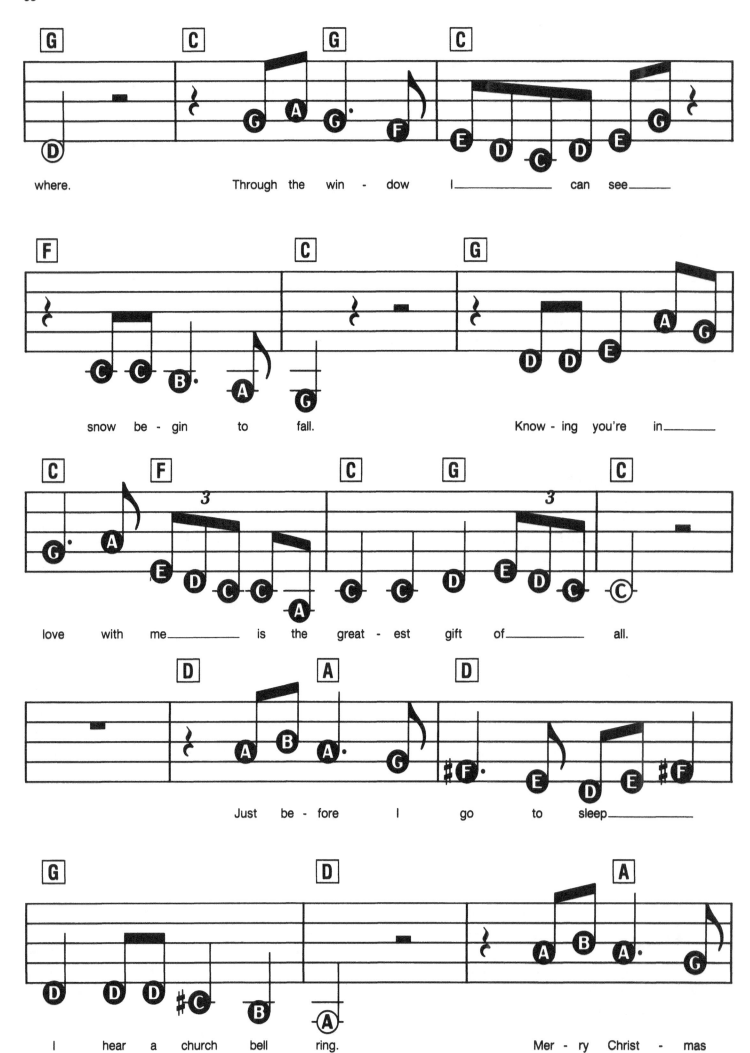

Happy Christmas, Little Friend

Registration 4
Rhythm: Waltz

Lyrics by Oscar Hammerstein II
Music by Richard Rodgers

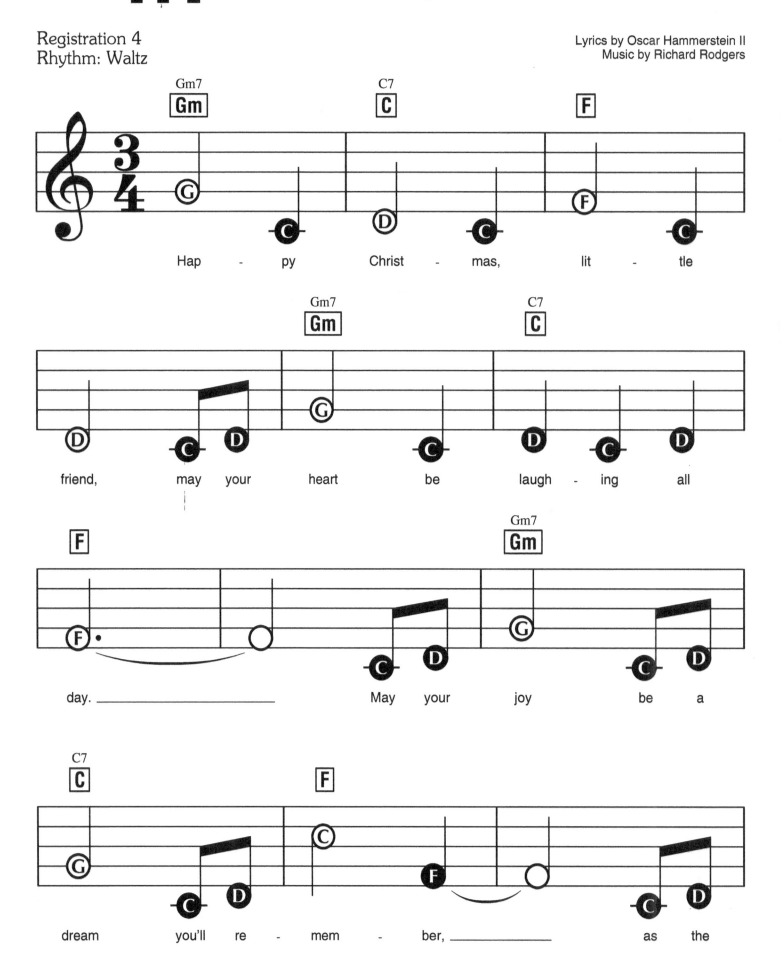

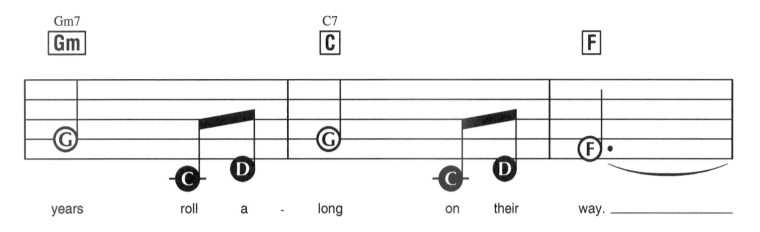

years   roll   a - long   on   their   way. _____

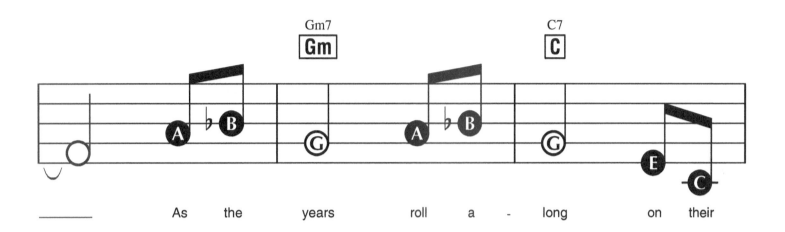

_____   As   the   years   roll   a - long   on   their

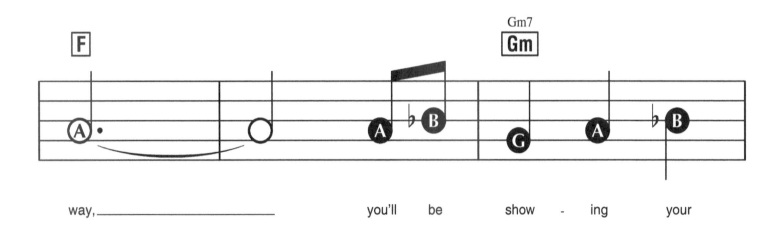

way, _____   you'll   be   show - ing   your

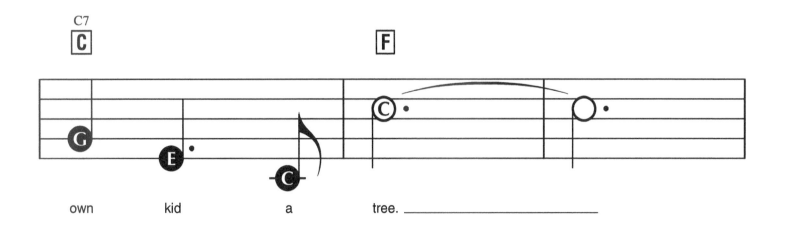

own   kid   a   tree. _____

64

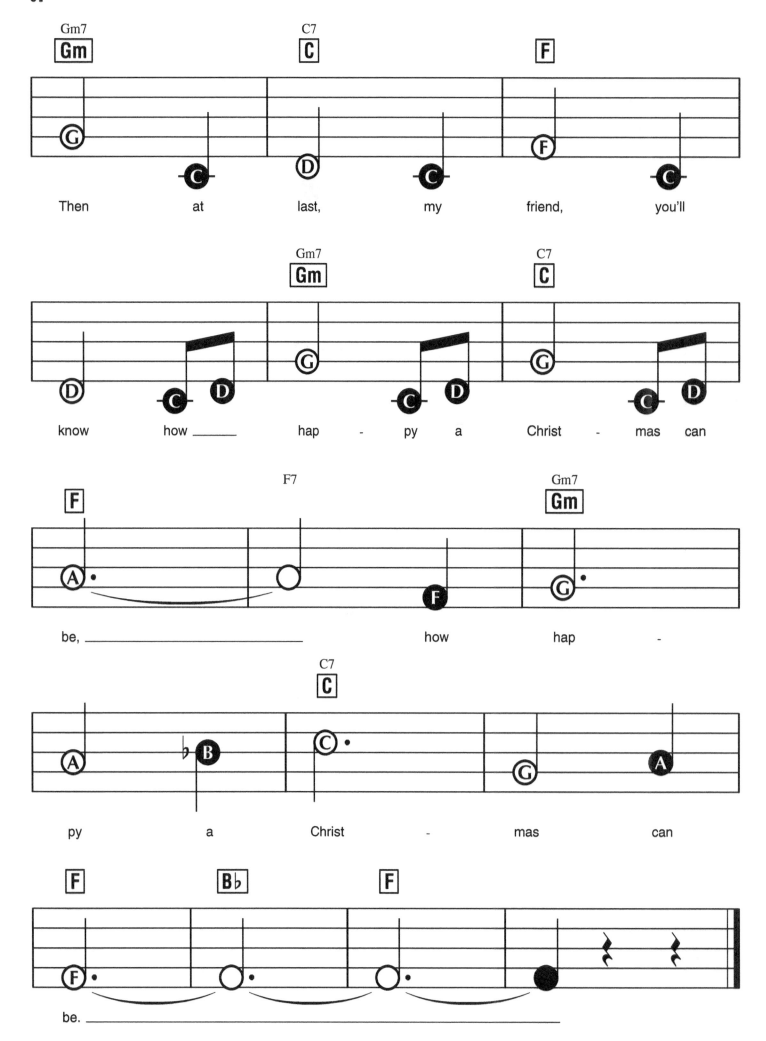

Happy Xmas
(War Is Over)

Registration 1
Rhythm: Slow Rock

Words and Music by John Lennon
and Yoko Ono

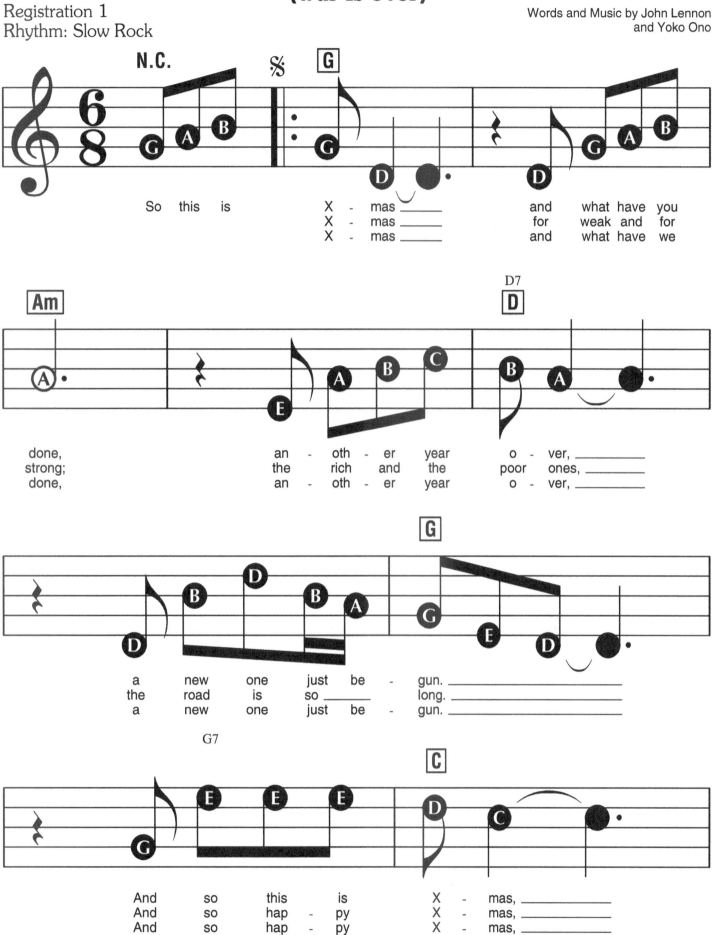

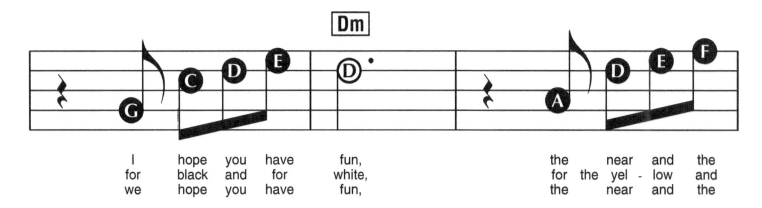

I hope you have fun, the near and the
for black and for white, for the yel - low and
we hope you have fun, the near and the

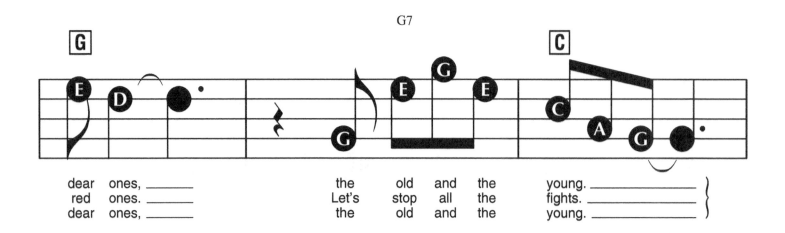

dear ones, _____ the old and the young. _____
red ones. _____ Let's stop all the fights. _____
dear ones, _____ the old and the young. _____

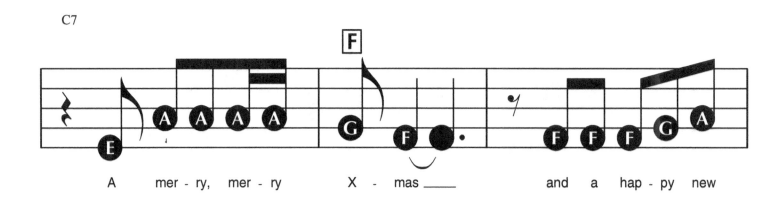

A mer - ry, mer - ry X - mas _____ and a hap - py new

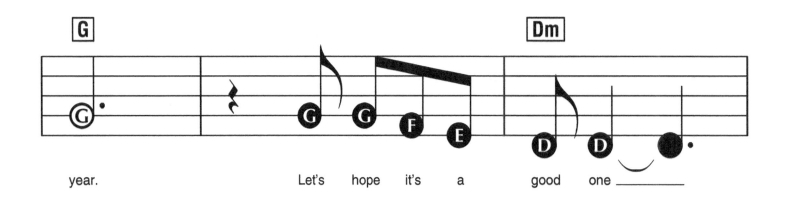

year. Let's hope it's a good one _____

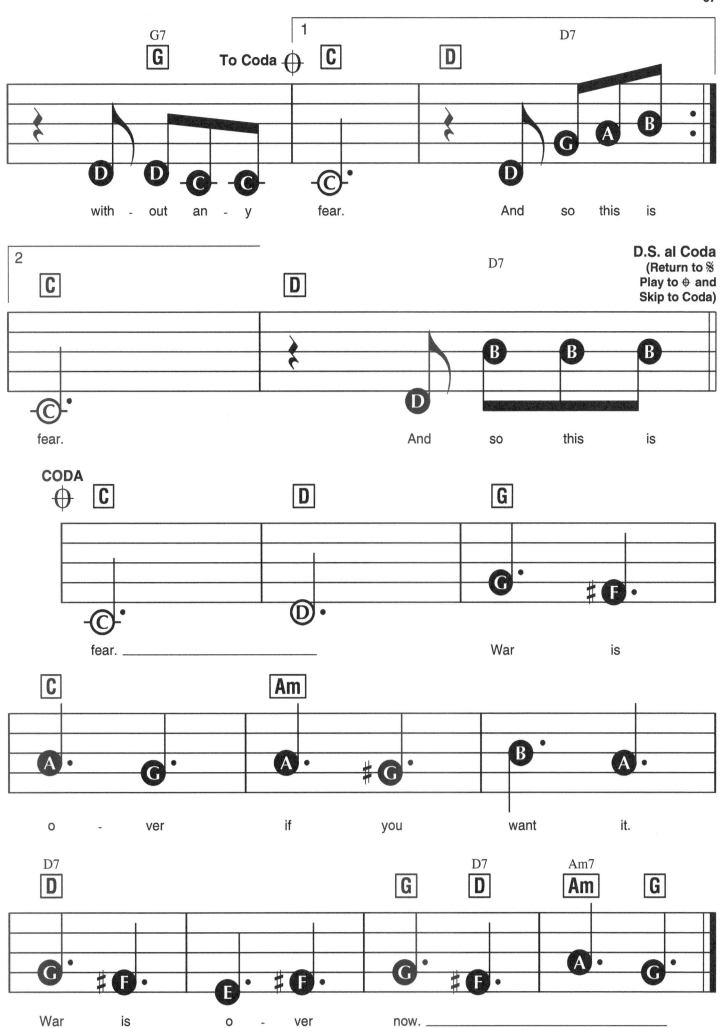

Happy Holiday
from the Motion Picture Irving Berlin's HOLIDAY INN

Registration 4
Rhythm: Fox Trot or Ballad

Words and Music by
Irving Berlin

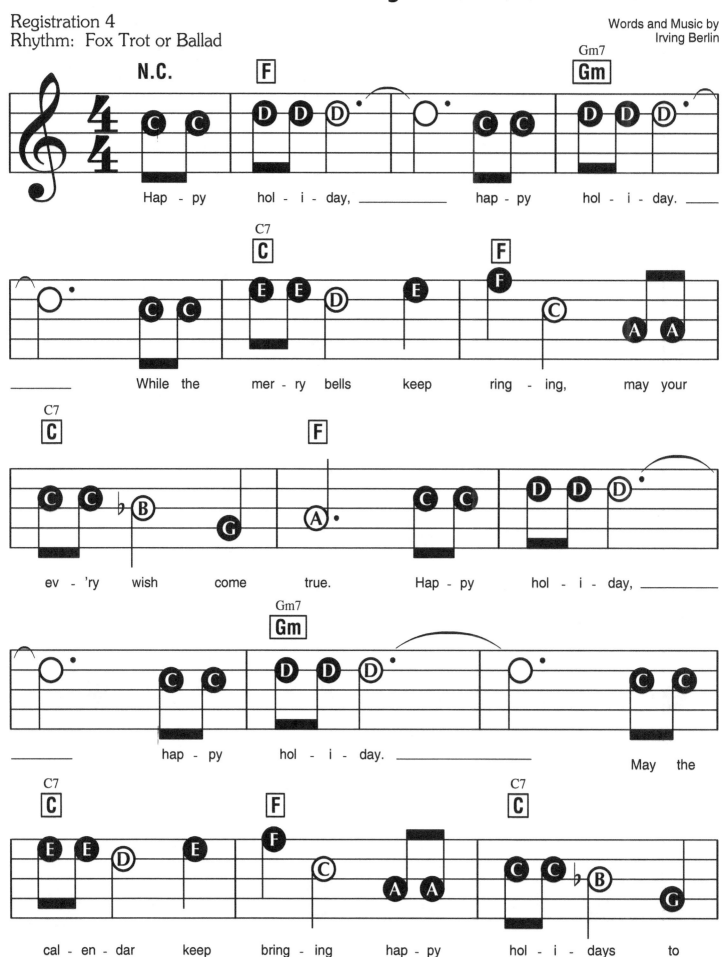

69

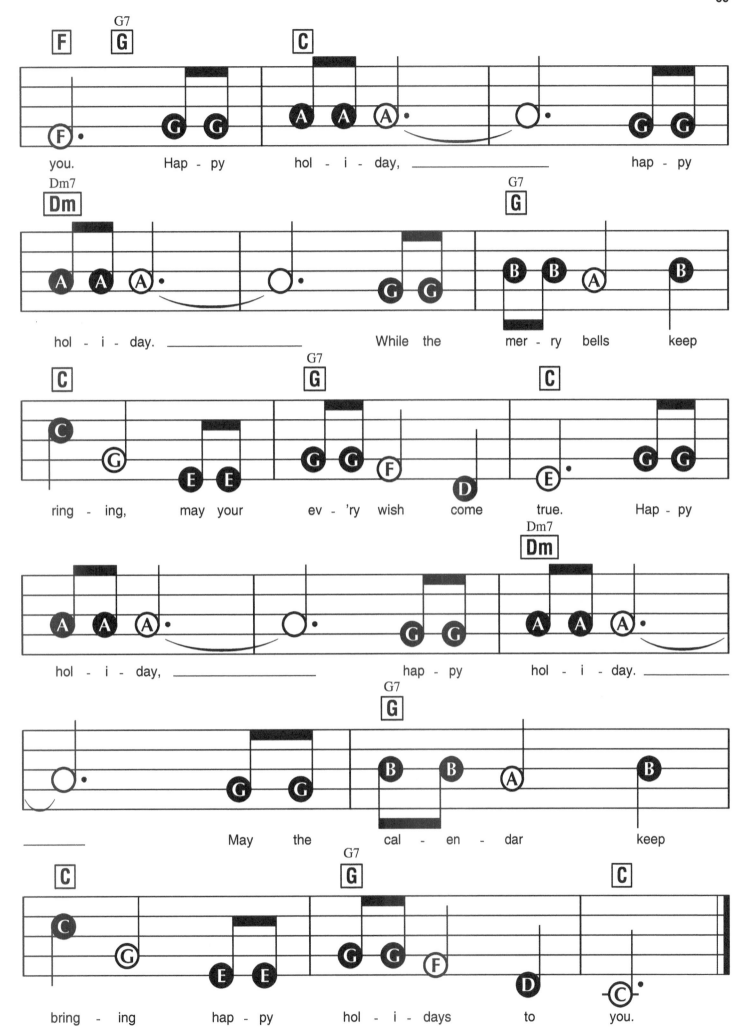

Hark! The Herald Angels Sing

Registration 5
Rhythm: None

Words by Charles Wesley
Altered by George Whitefield
Music by Felix Mendelssohn-Bartholdy
Arranged by William H. Cummings

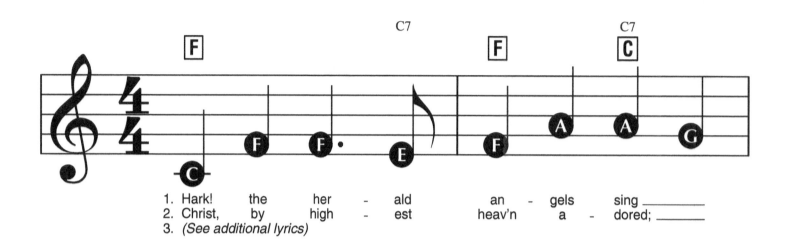

1. Hark! the her - ald an - gels sing _____
2. Christ, by high - est heav'n a - dored; _____
3. *(See additional lyrics)*

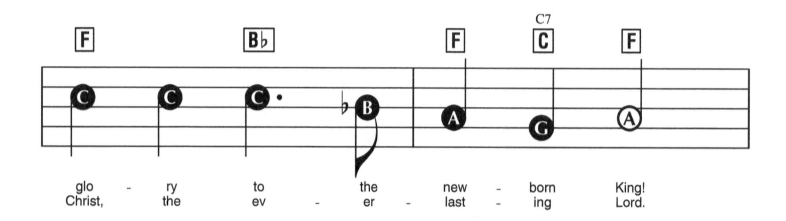

glo - ry to the new - born King!
Christ, the ev - er - last - ing Lord.

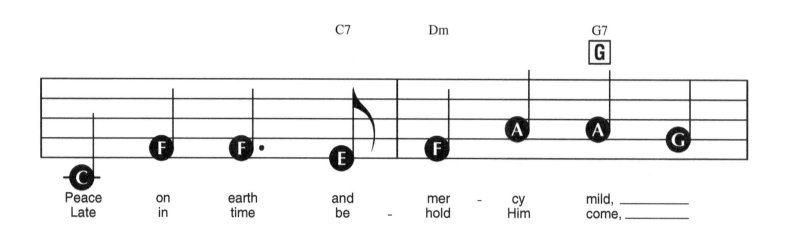

Peace on earth and mer - cy mild, _____
Late in time be - hold Him come, _____

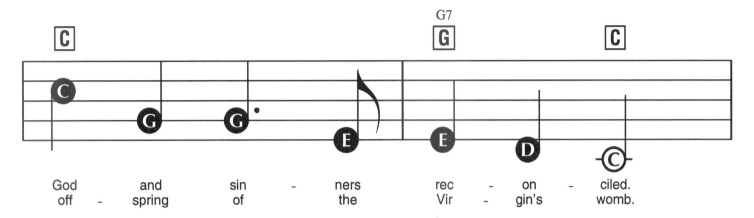

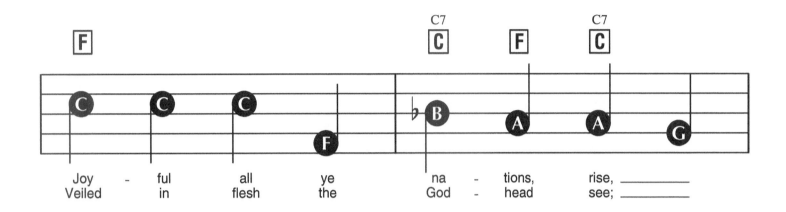

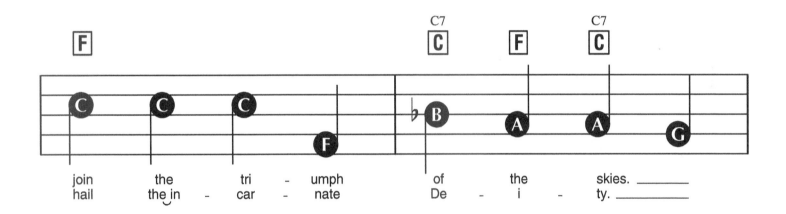

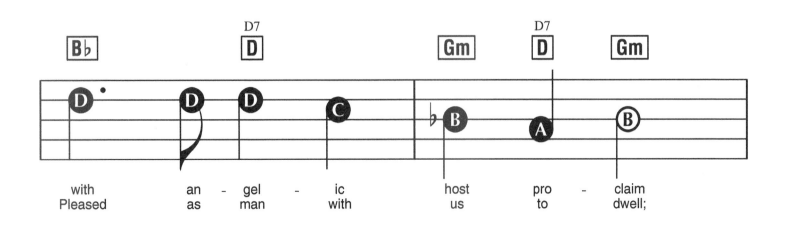

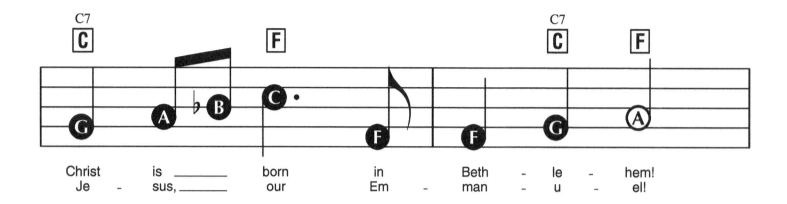

Christ is _____ born in Beth - le - hem!
Je - sus, _____ our Em - man - u - el!

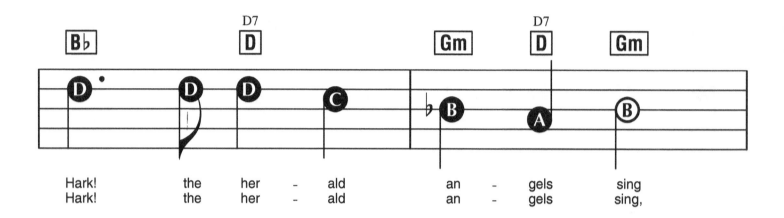

Hark! the her - ald an - gels sing
Hark! the her - ald an - gels sing,

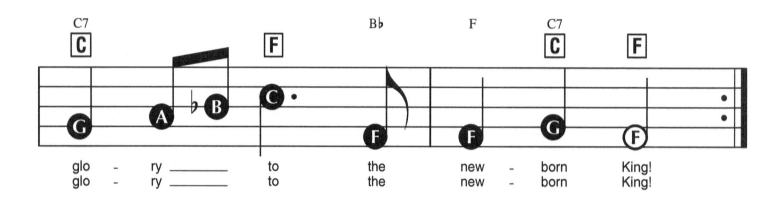

glo - ry _____ to the new - born King!
glo - ry _____ to the new - born King!

Additional Lyrics

3. Hail, the heaven-born Prince of Peace!
Hail, the Sun of Righteousness!
Light and life to all He brings,
Risen with healing in His wings.
Mild He lays His glory by,
Born that man no more may die.
Born to raise the sons of earth,
Born to give them second birth.

Hark! the herald angels sing
Glory to the newborn King!

Here Comes Santa Claus
(Right Down Santa Claus Lane)

Registration 4
Rhythm: Swing

Words and Music by Gene Autry
and Oakley Haldeman

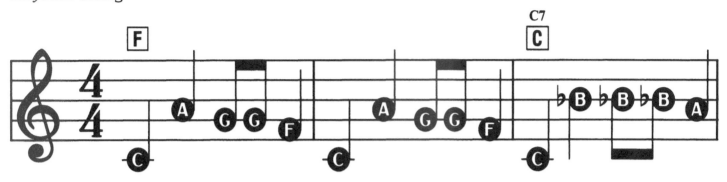

Here comes San - ta Claus! Here comes San - ta Claus! Right down San - ta Claus

Lane!

1. Vix - en and Blitz - en and all his rein - deer are
2. He's got a bag that is filled with toys for the

pull - ing on the rein.
boys and girls a - gain.

Bells are ring - ing,
Hear those sleigh - bells

chil - dren sing - ing, all is mer - ry and bright.
jin - gle jan - gle, what a beau - ti - ful sight.

74

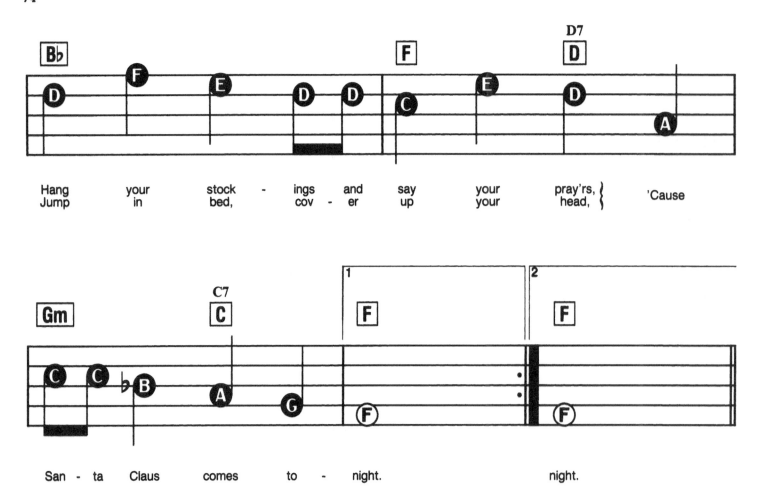

Hang your stock - ings and say your pray'rs, } 'Cause
Jump in bed, cov - er up your head,

San - ta Claus comes to - night.   night.

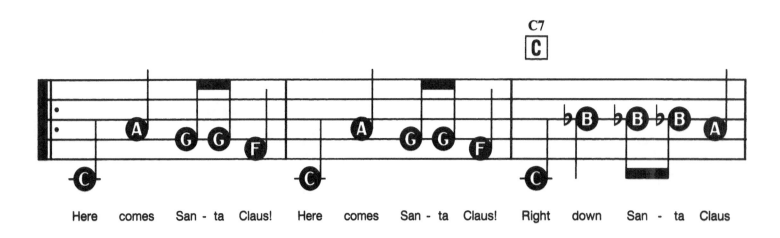

Here comes San - ta Claus! Here comes San - ta Claus! Right down San - ta Claus

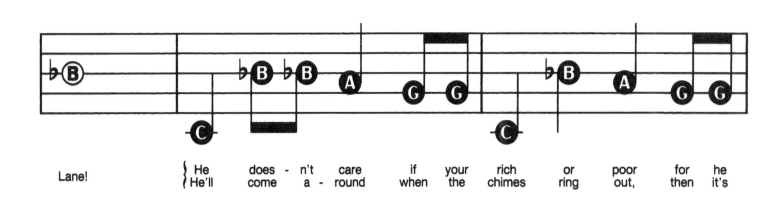

Lane!   { He does - n't care if your rich or poor, for he
          { He'll come a - round when the chimes ring out, then it's

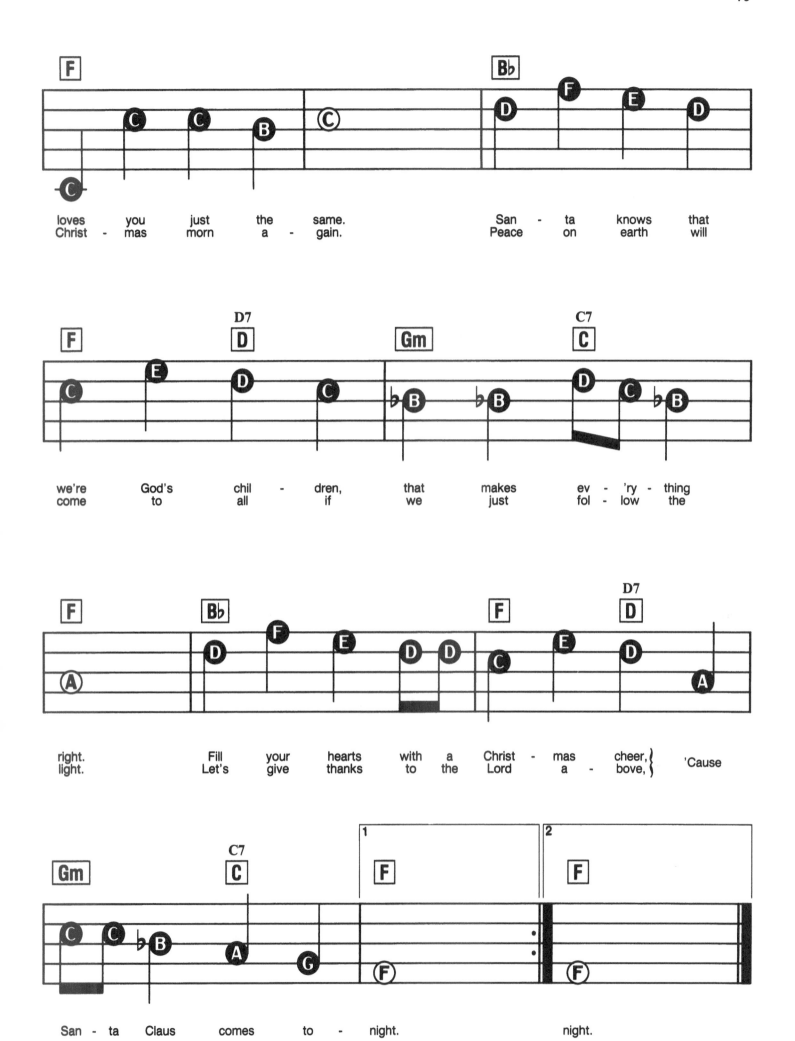

I Heard the Bells on Christmas Day

Registration 7
Rhythm: Ballad or Fox Trot

Words by Henry Wadsworth Longfellow
Music by John Baptiste Calkin

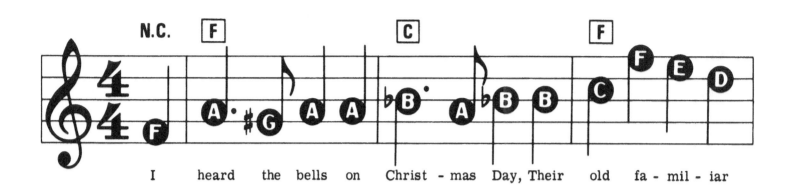

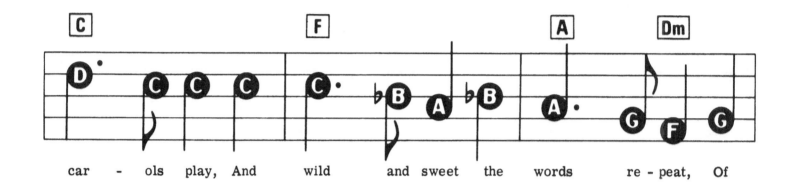

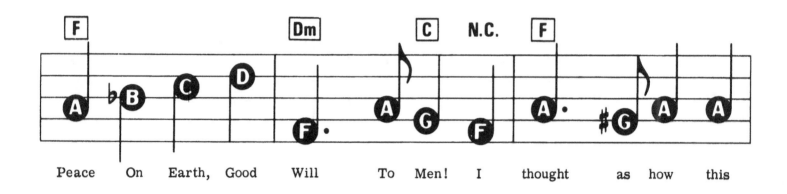

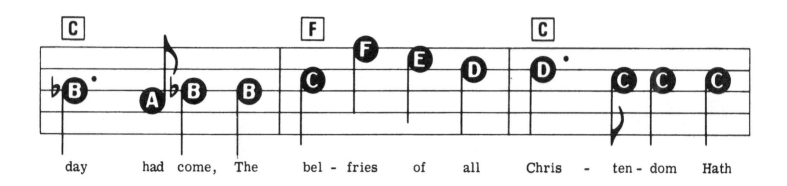

77

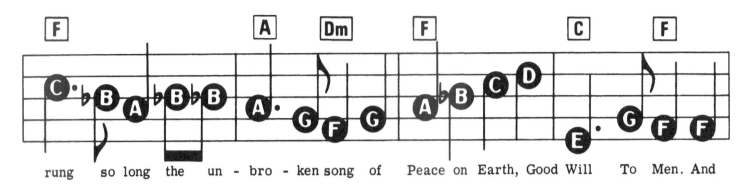

rung   so long   the   un - bro - ken song   of   Peace on Earth, Good Will   To   Men. And

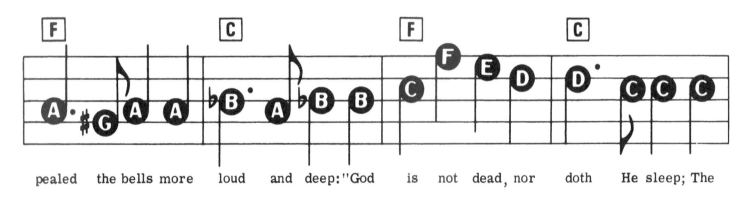

in   des-pair I   bowed   my head:"There is   no peace on   earth," I   said "For

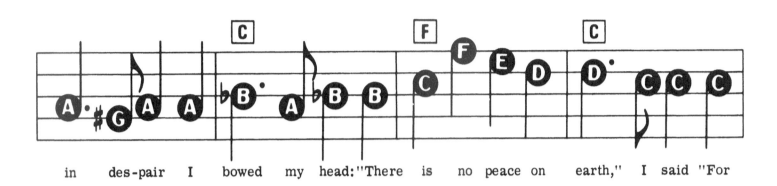

hate   is strong and   mocks   the song   of   Peace On Earth, Good   Will   To   Men." Then

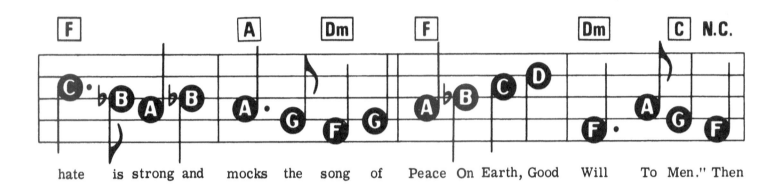

pealed   the bells more   loud   and deep:"God   is   not dead, nor   doth   He sleep; The

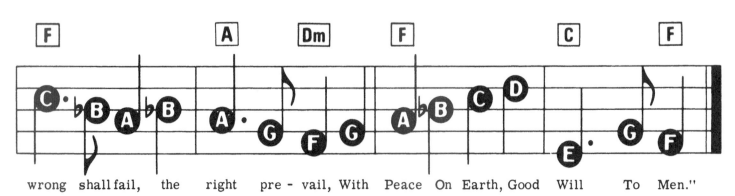

wrong shall fail,   the   right pre - vail, With Peace On Earth, Good Will   To   Men."

I Saw Mommy Kissing Santa Claus

Registration 5
Rhythm: Fox Trot or Swing

Words and Music by
Tommie Connor

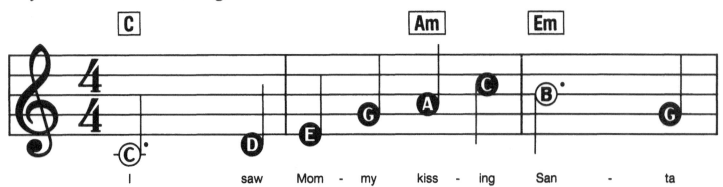

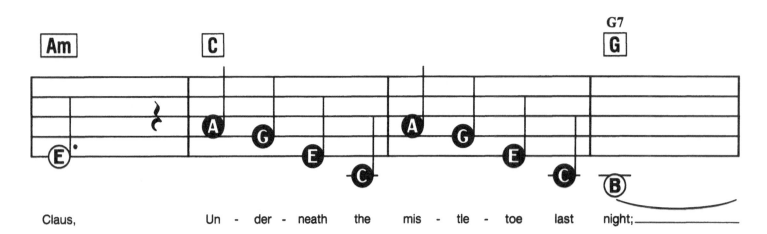

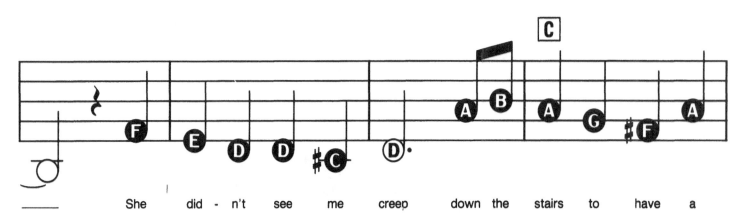

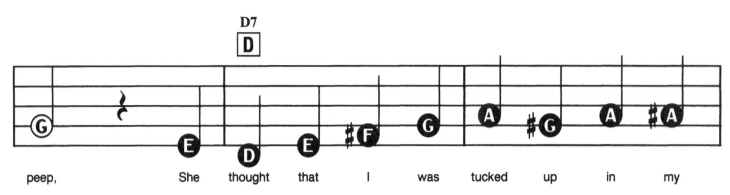

I'll Be Home for Christmas

Registration 1
Rhythm: Fox Trot

Words and Music by Kim Gannon
and Walter Kent

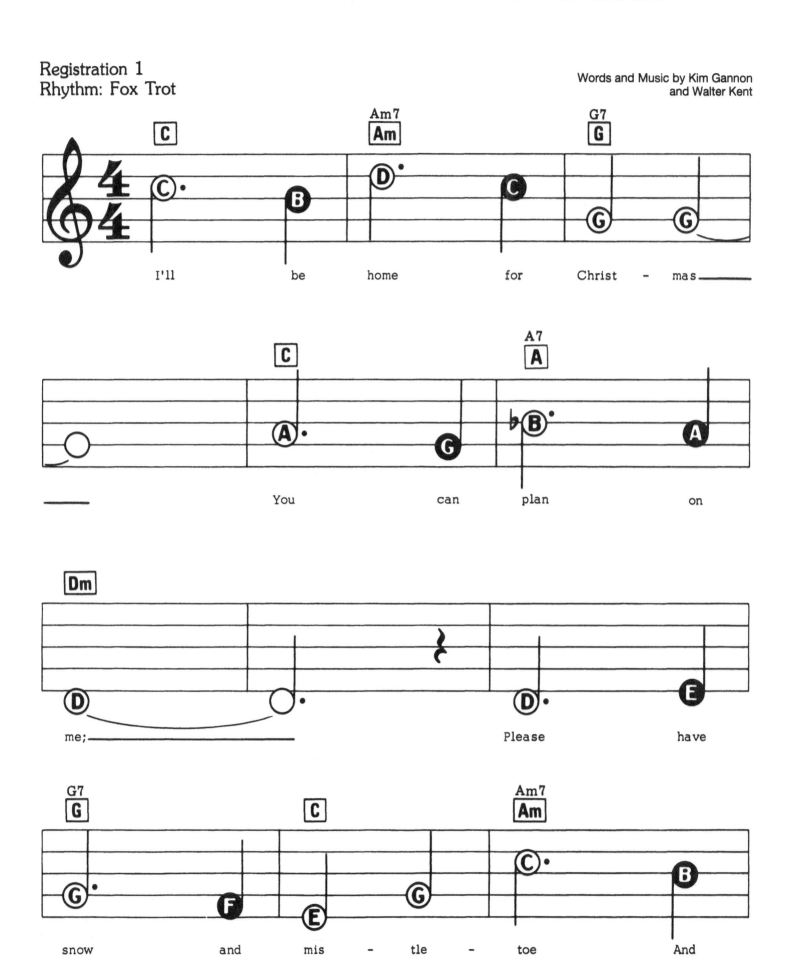

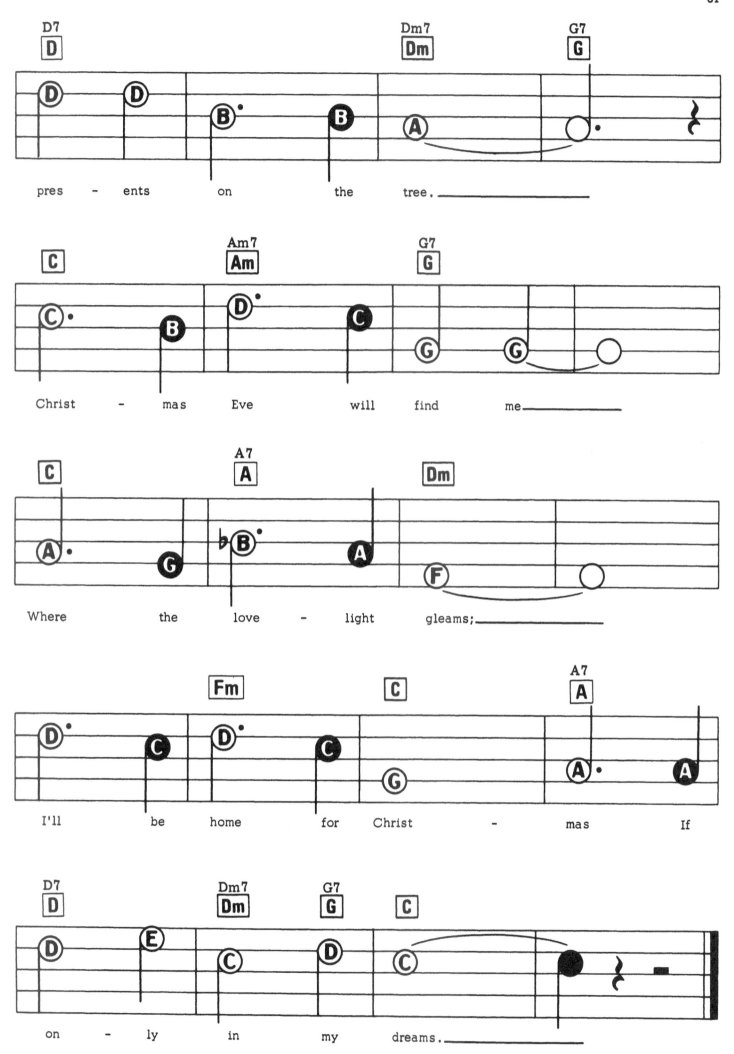

I Still Believe in Santa Claus

Registration 8
Rhythm: 8 Beat or Rock

Words and Music by Maurice Starr
and Al Lancellotti

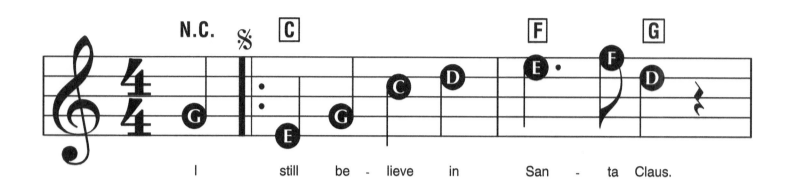

I still be - lieve in San - ta Claus.

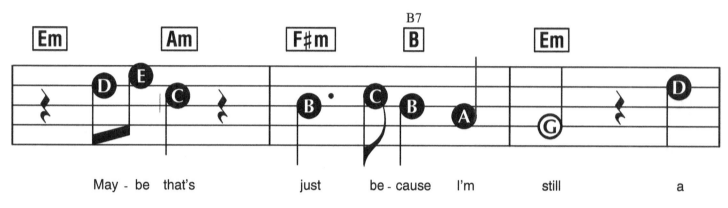

May - be that's just be - cause I'm still a

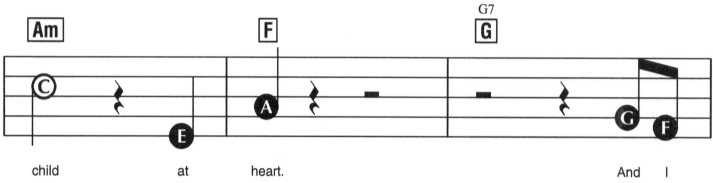

child at heart. And I

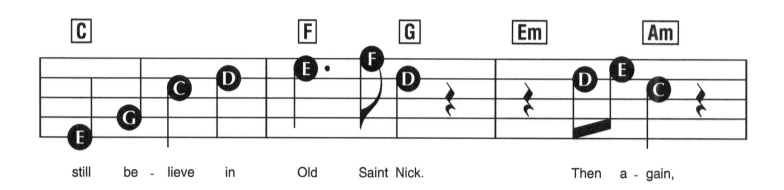

still be - lieve in Old Saint Nick. Then a - gain,

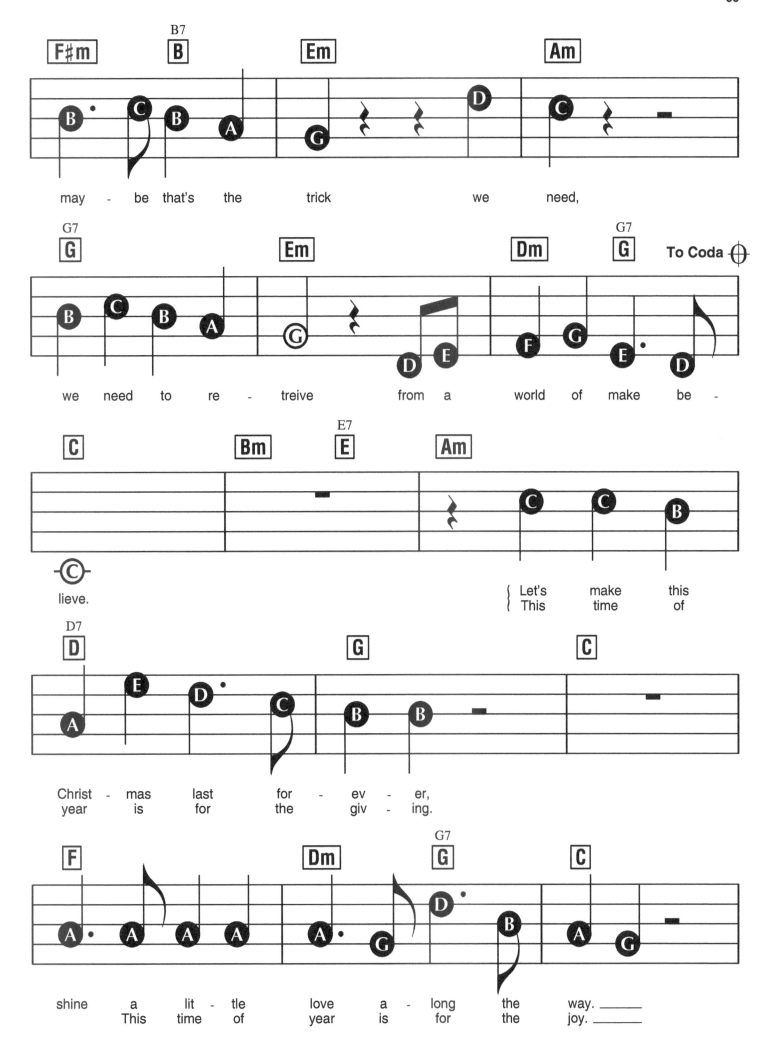

84

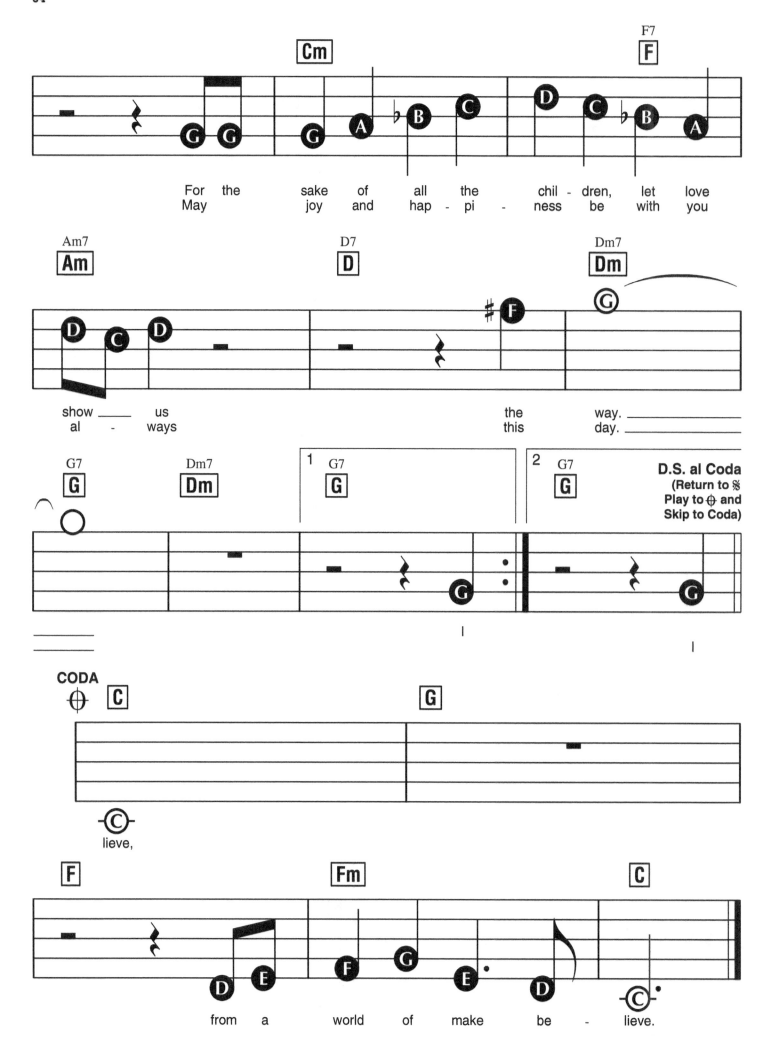

It Must Have Been the Mistletoe
(Our First Christmas)

Registration 1
Rhythm: 6/8 or Waltz

By Justin Wilde
and Doug Konecky

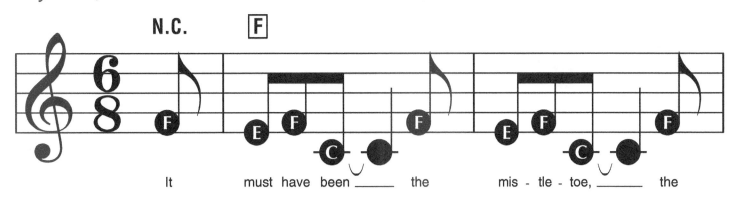

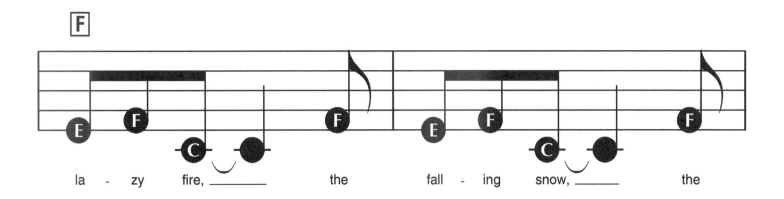

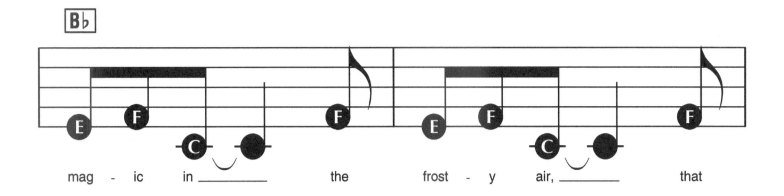

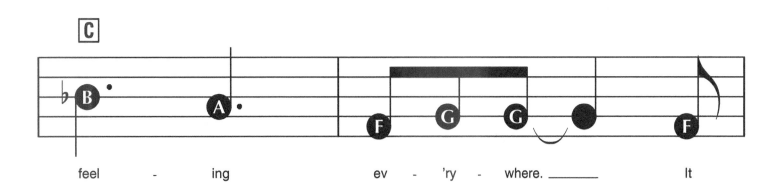

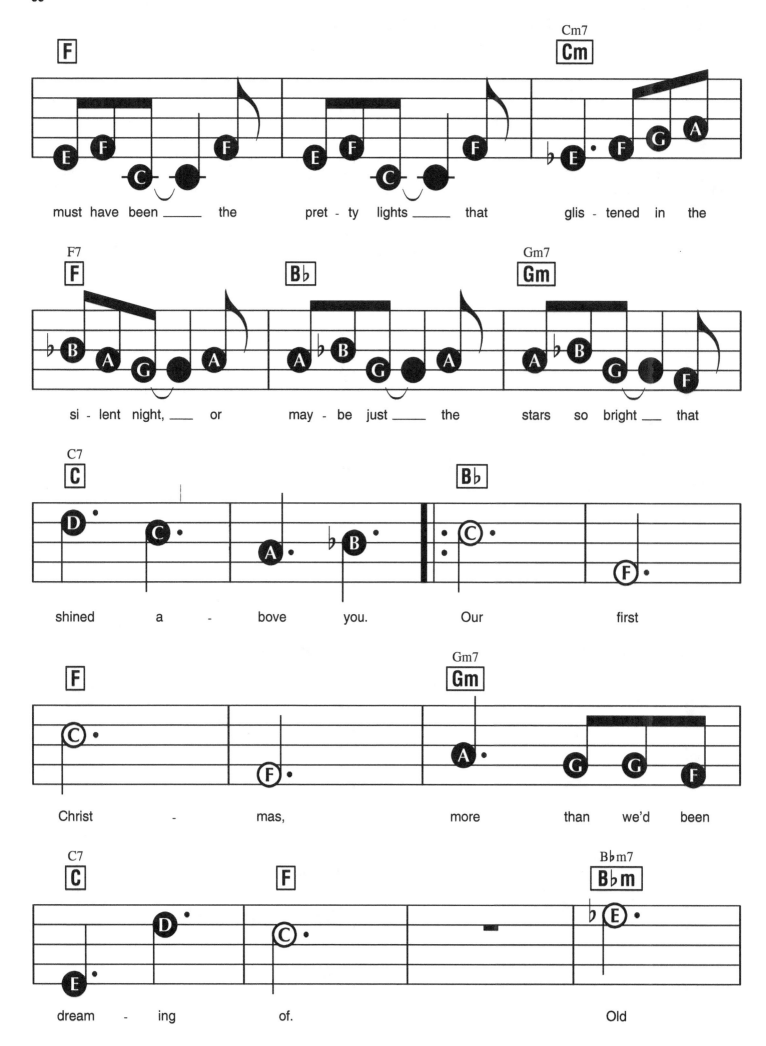

87

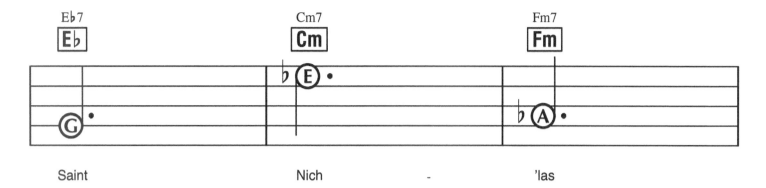

Saint   Nich   -   'las

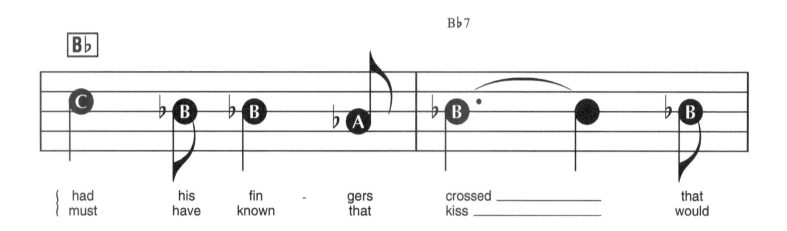

had   his   fin - gers   crossed _____   that
must   have   known   that   kiss _____   would

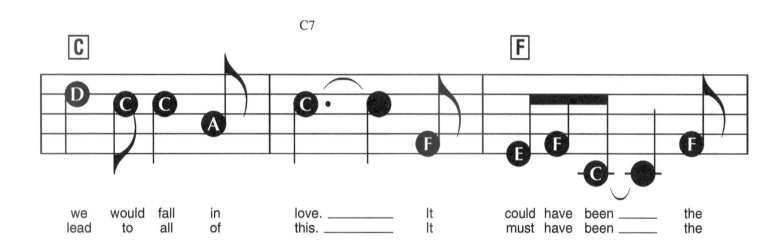

we   would fall   in   love. _____ It   could have been _____ the
lead   to   all   of   this. _____ It   must   have been _____ the

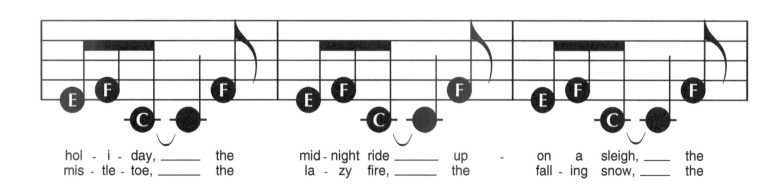

hol - i - day, _____ the   mid - night ride _____ up - on a sleigh, _____ the
mis - tle - toe, _____ the   la - zy fire, _____ the   fall - ing snow, _____ the

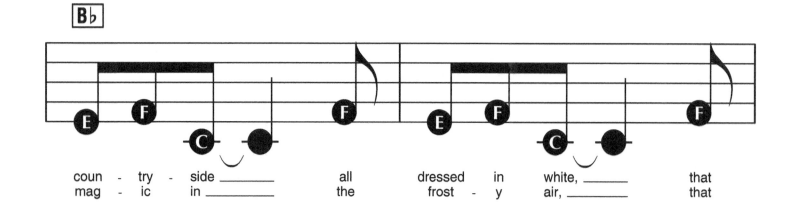

coun - try - side _____ all dressed in white, _____ that
mag - ic in _____ the frost - y air, _____ that

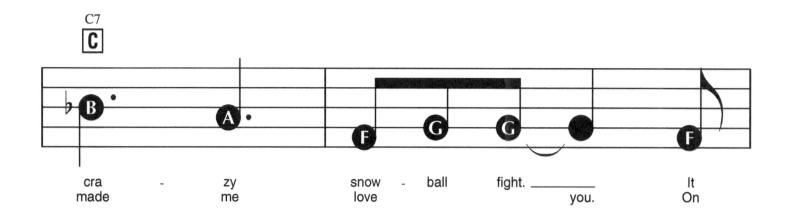

cra - zy snow - ball fight. _____ It
made me love you. On

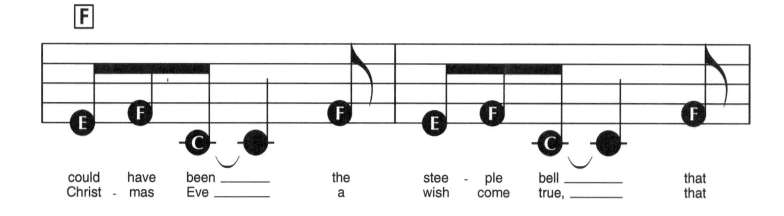

could have been _____ the stee - ple bell _____ that
Christ - mas Eve _____ a wish come true, _____ that

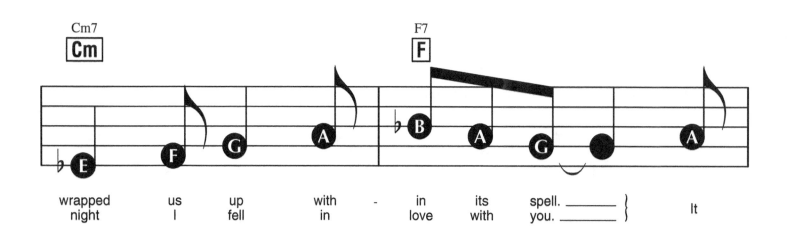

wrapped us up with - in its spell. _____ } It
night I fell in love with you. _____

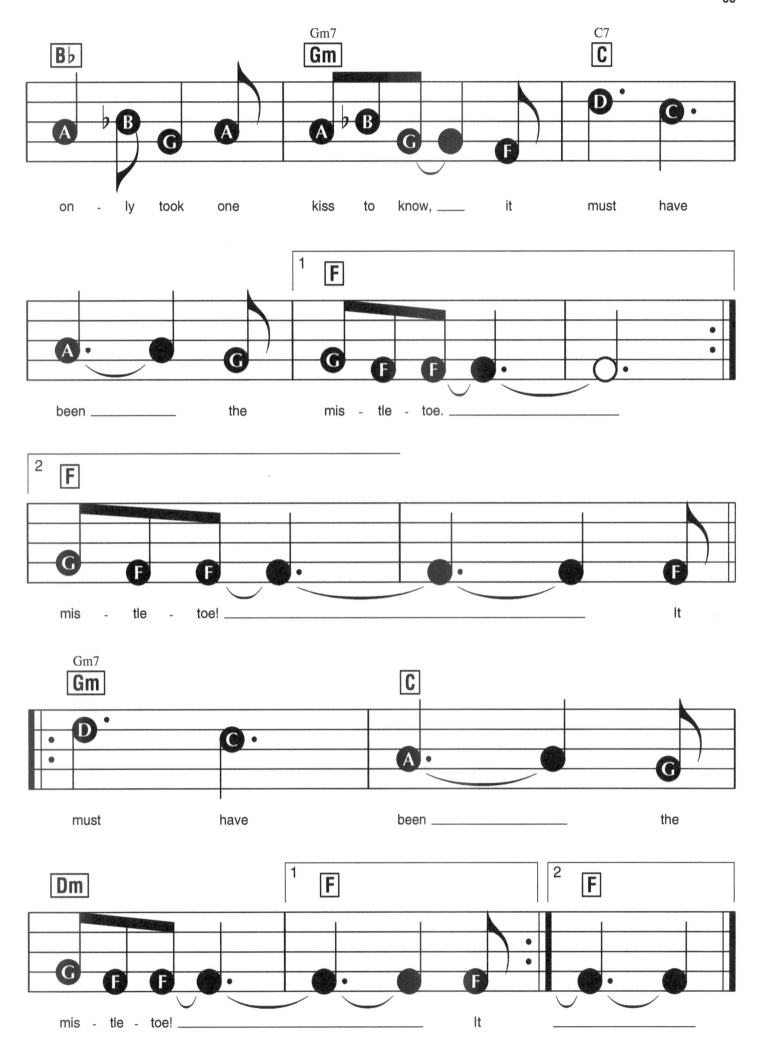

It's Beginning to Look Like Christmas

Registration 5
Rhythm: Fox Trot or Shuffle

By Meredith Willson

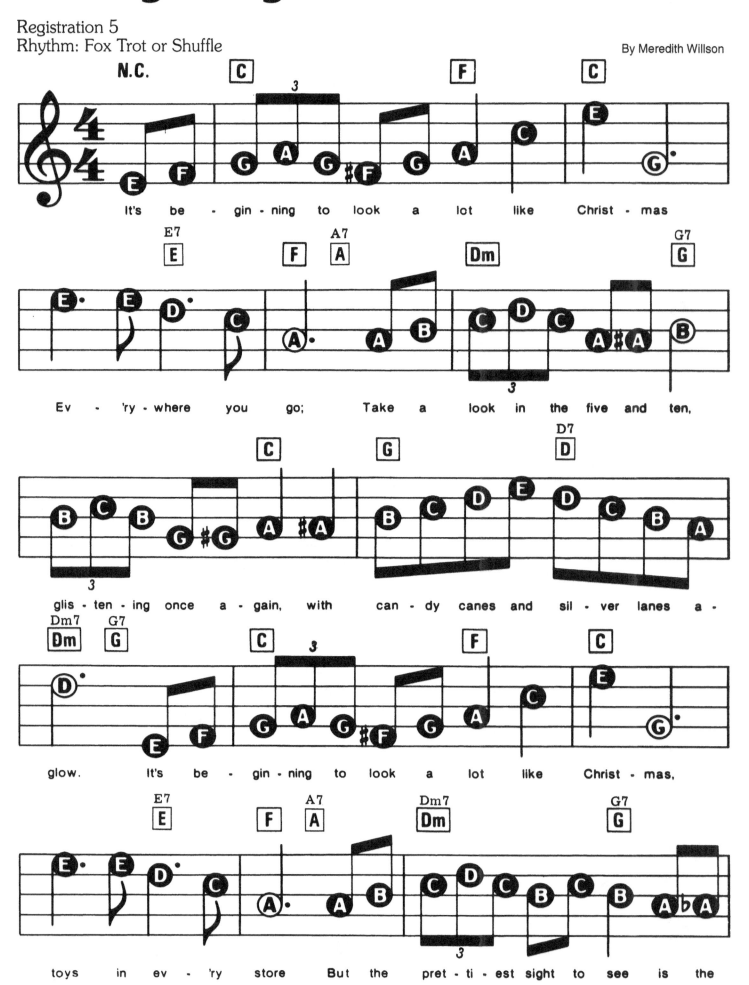

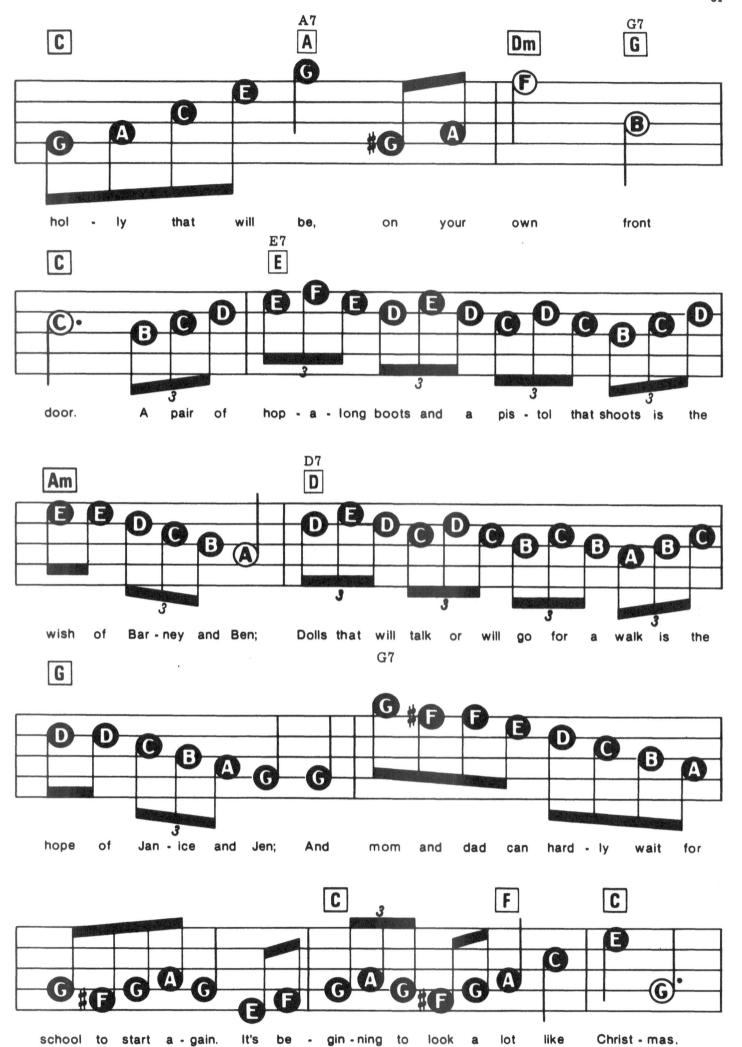

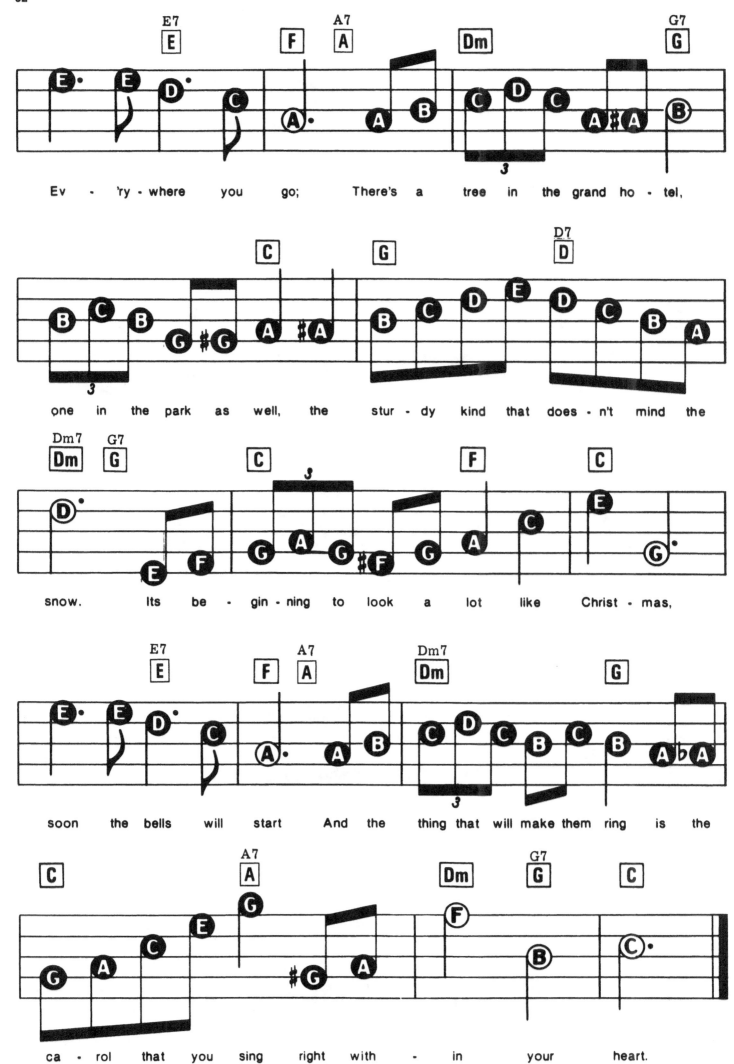

It's Christmas in New York

Registration 2
Rhythm: Ballad or Fox Trot

Words and Music by
Billy Butt

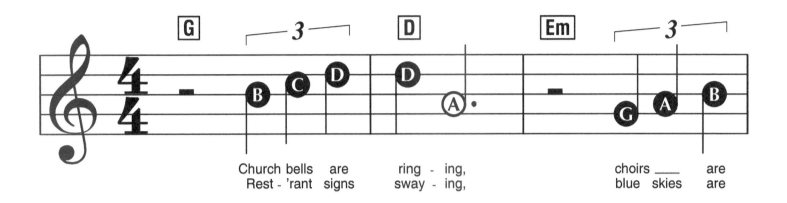

Church bells are ring - ing,   choirs ___ are
Rest - 'rant signs sway - ing,   blue skies are

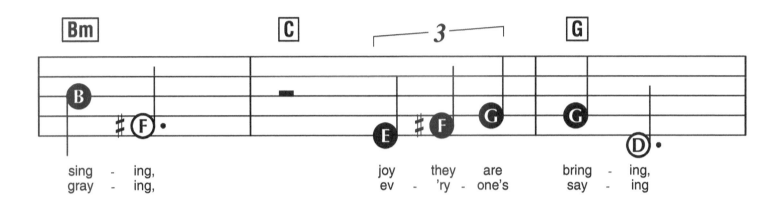

sing - ing,   joy they are   bring - ing,
gray - ing,   ev - 'ry one's   say - ing

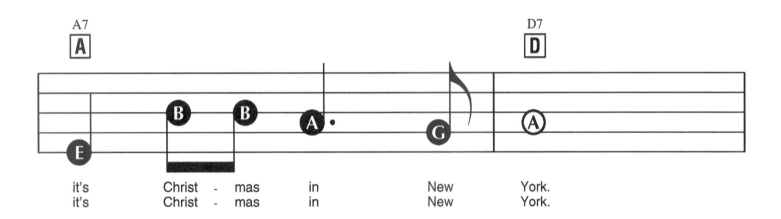

it's Christ - mas in   New York.
it's Christ - mas in   New New York.

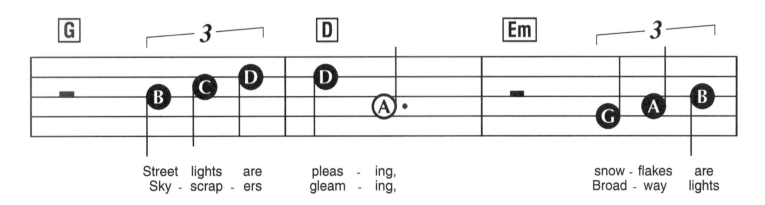

Street lights are pleas - ing,   snow - flakes are
Sky - scrap - ers gleam - ing,   Broad - way lights

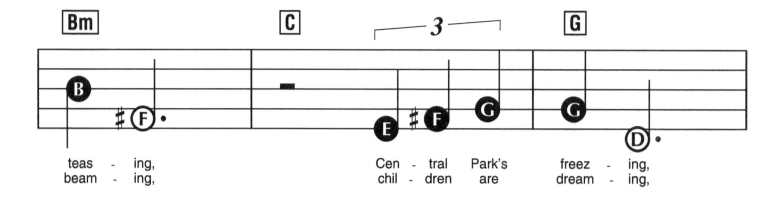

teas - ing, Cen - tral Park's freez - ing,
beam - ing, chil - dren are dream - ing,

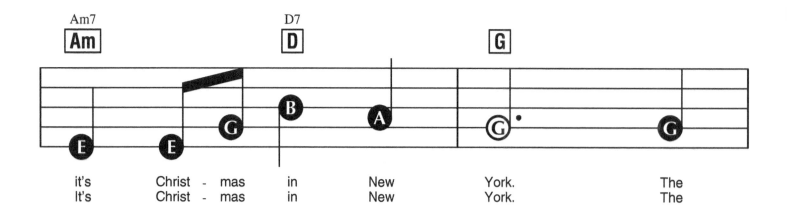

it's Christ - mas in New York. The
It's Christ - mas in New New York. The

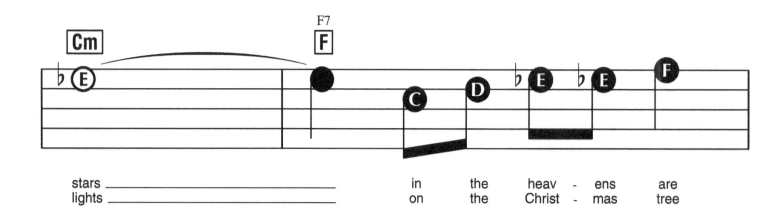

stars _____ in the heav - ens are
lights _____ on the Christ - mas tree

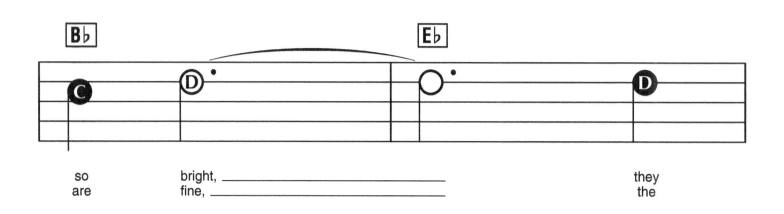

so bright, _____ they
are fine, _____ the

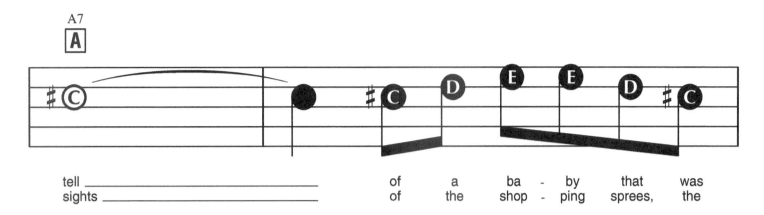

tell ___ of a ba - by that was
sights ___ of the shop - ping sprees, was the

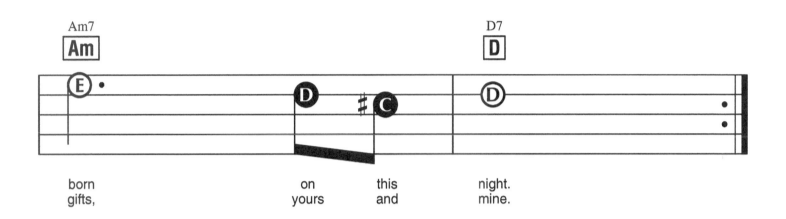

born on this night.
gifts, yours and mine.

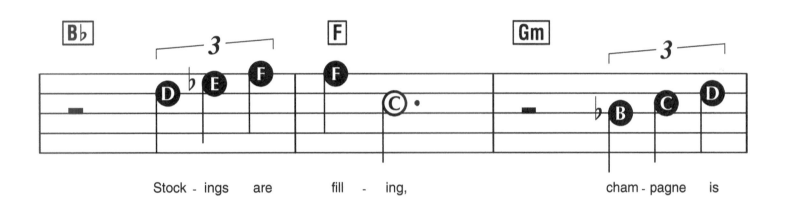

Stock - ings are fill - ing, cham - pagne is

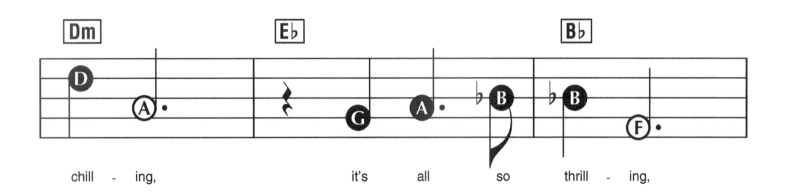

chill - ing, it's all so thrill - ing,

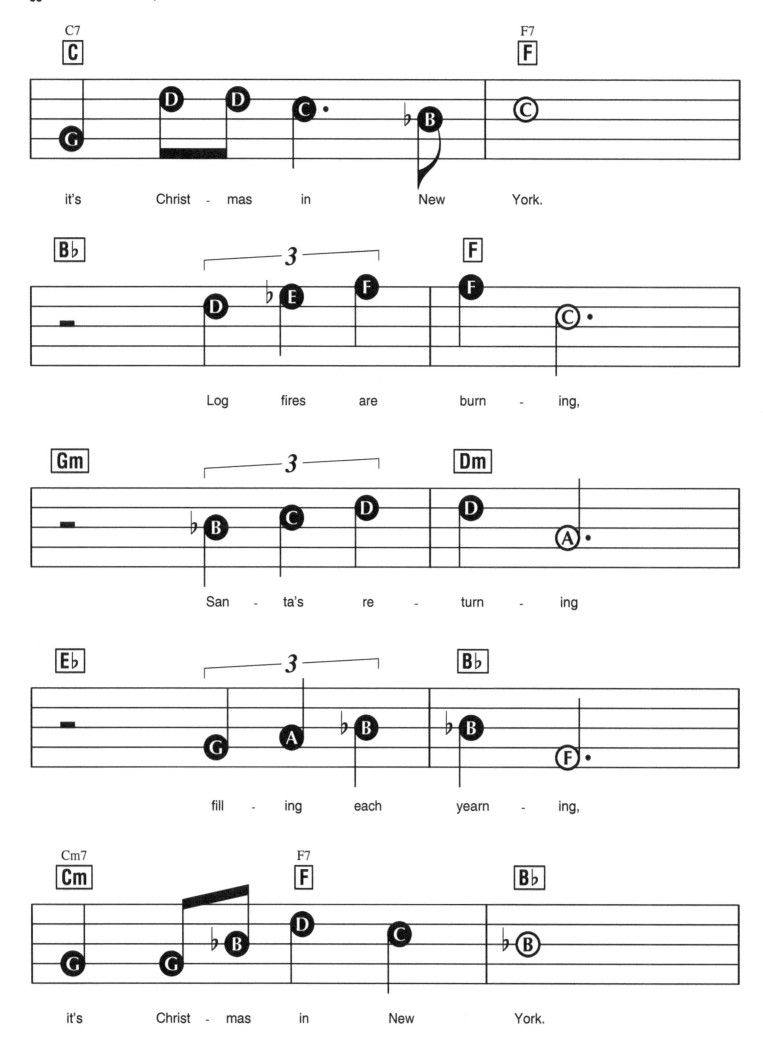

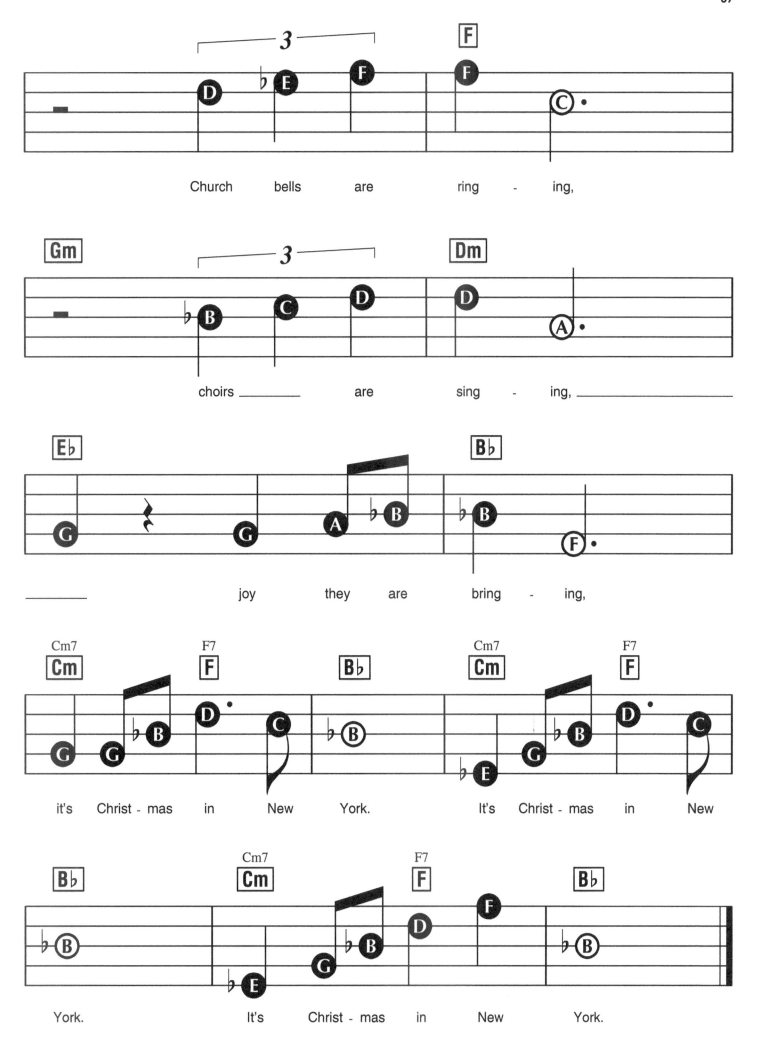

Jingle Bells

Registration 5
Rhythm: Fox Trot or Swing

Words and Music by
J. Pierpont

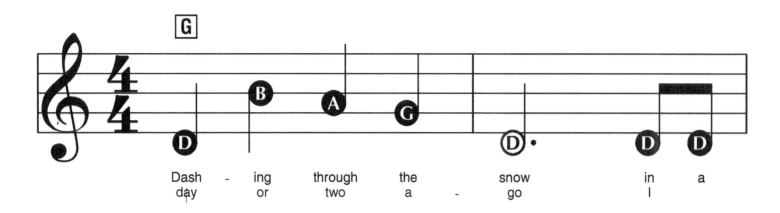

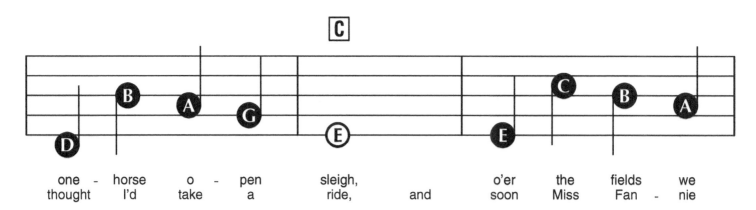

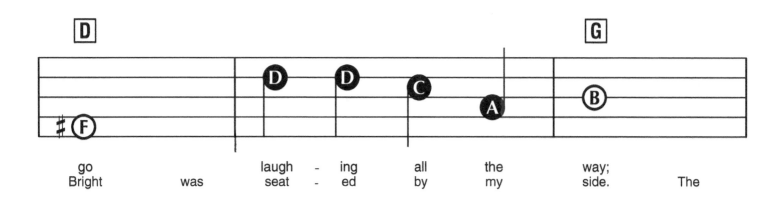

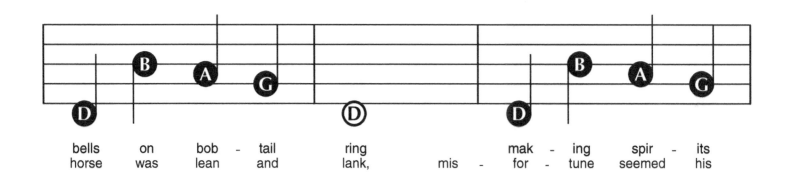

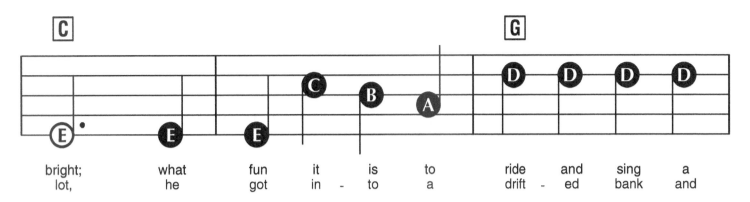

bright;   what   fun   it   is   to   ride   and   sing   a
lot,   he   got   in - to   a   drift - ed   bank   and

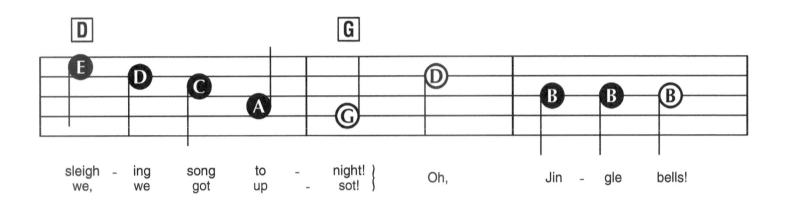

sleigh - ing   song   to - night! }   Oh,   Jin - gle   bells!
we,   we   got   up - sot!

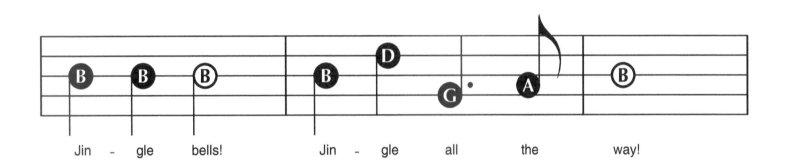

Jin - gle   bells!   Jin - gle   all   the   way!

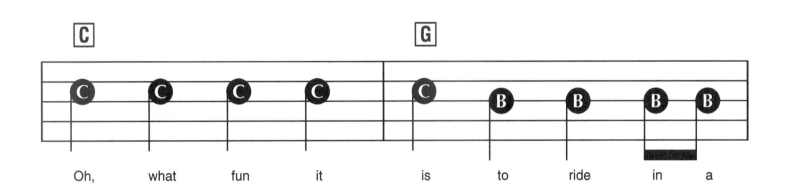

Oh,   what   fun   it   is   to   ride   in   a

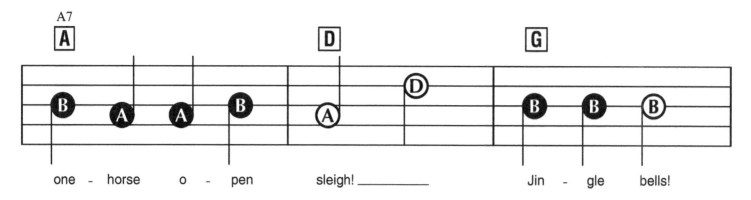

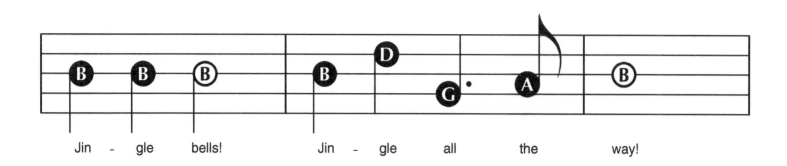

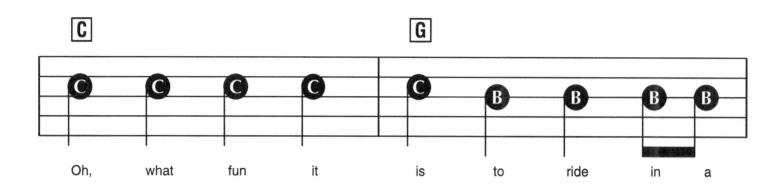

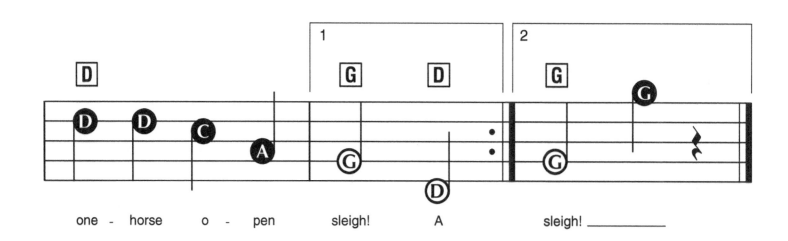

Merry Christmas, Darling

Registration 9
Rhythm: 4/4 Ballad

Words and Music by Richard Carpenter
and Frank Pooler

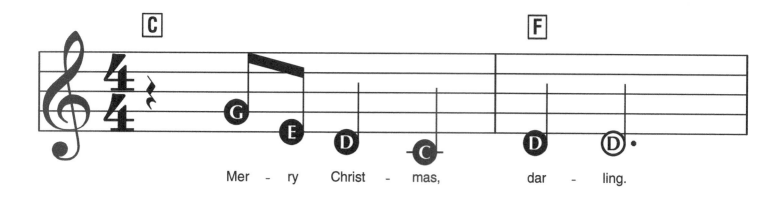

Mer - ry Christ - mas, dar - ling.

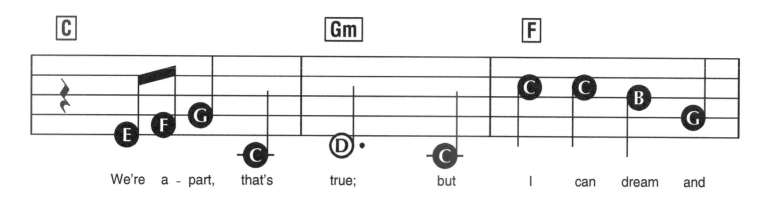

We're a - part, that's true; but I can dream and

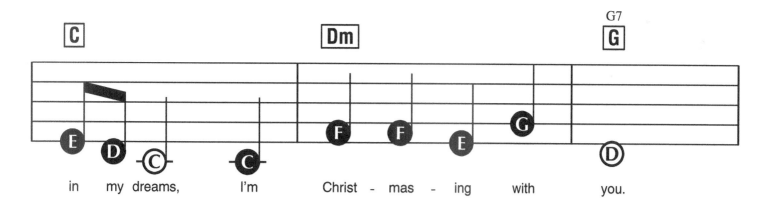

in my dreams, I'm Christ - mas - ing with you.

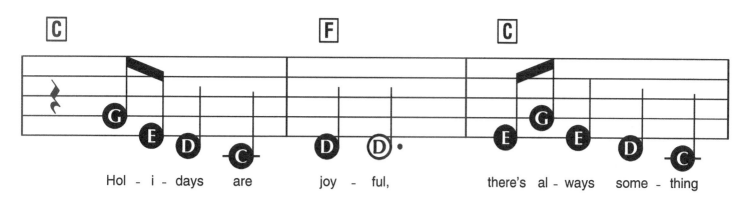

Hol - i - days are joy - ful, there's al - ways some - thing

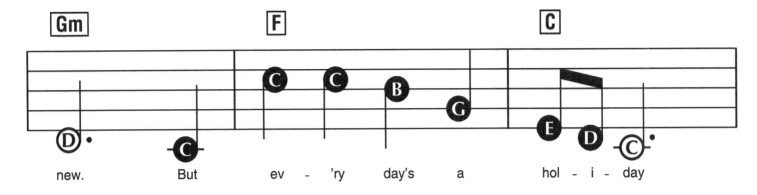

new.   But   ev - 'ry   day's   a   hol - i - day

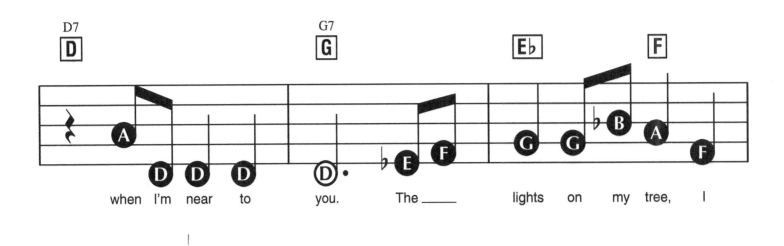

when I'm near   to   you.   The _____   lights on my tree, I

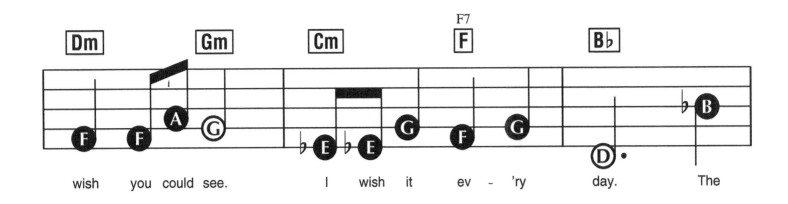

wish you could see.   I wish it ev - 'ry   day.   The

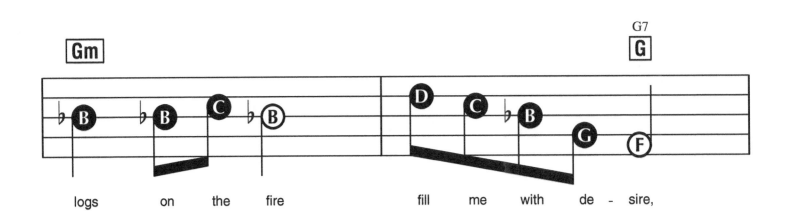

logs   on   the   fire   fill me with de - sire,

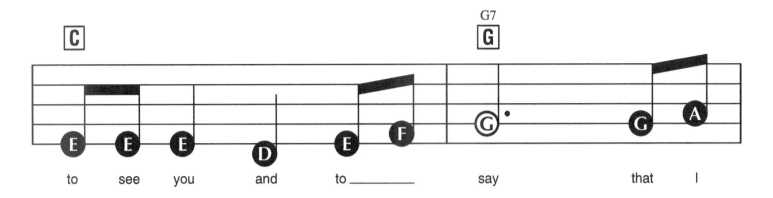

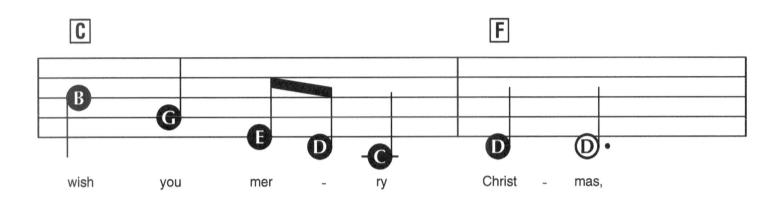

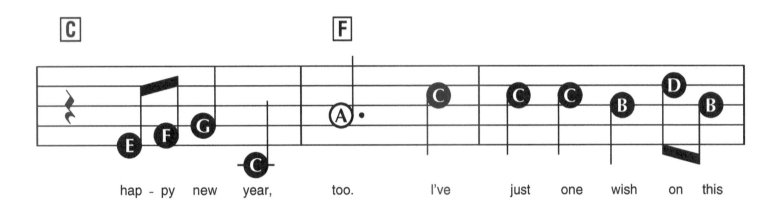

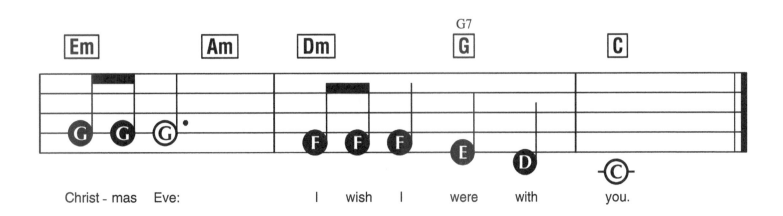

Joy to the World

Registration 2
Rhythm: None

Words by Isaac Watts
Music by George Frideric Handel
Arranged by Lowell Mason

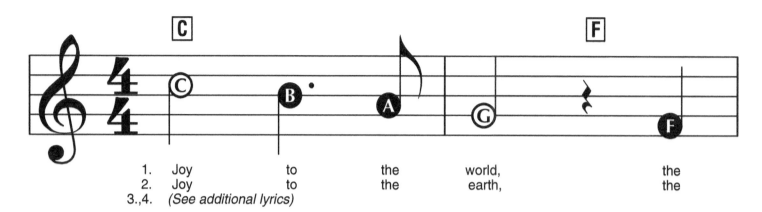

1. Joy   to   the   world,   the
2. Joy   to   the   earth,   the
3.,4. *(See additional lyrics)*

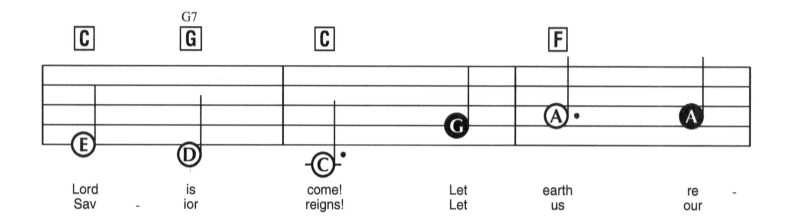

Lord   is   come!   Let   earth   re -
Sav - ior   reigns!   Let   us   our

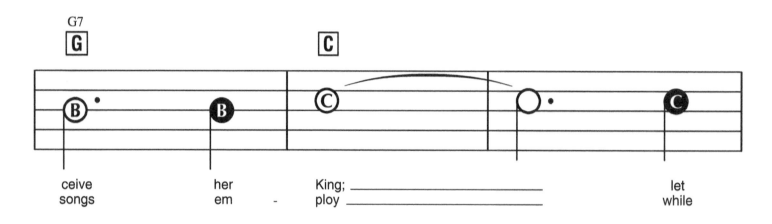

ceive   her   King; _____   let
songs   em - ploy _____   while

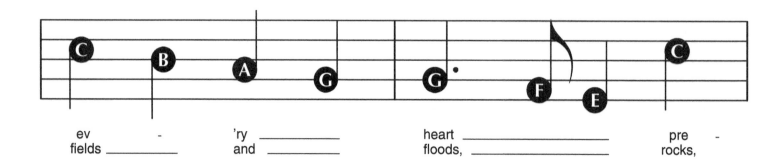

ev - 'ry _____ and _____ heart _____ pre -
fields _____ and _____ floods, _____ rocks,

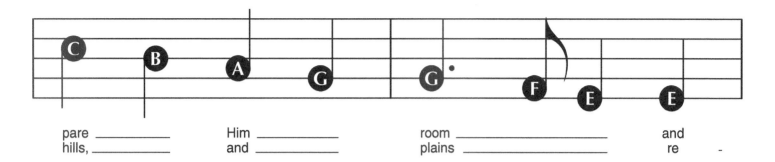

pare _____ Him _____ room _____ and
hills, _____ and _____ plains _____ re -

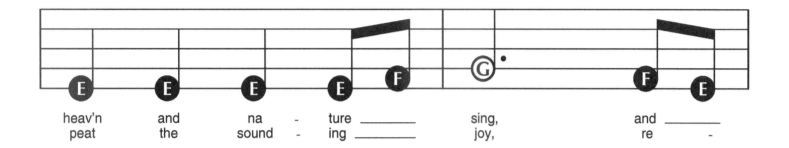

heav'n and na - ture _____ sing, and _____
peat the sound - ing _____ joy, re -

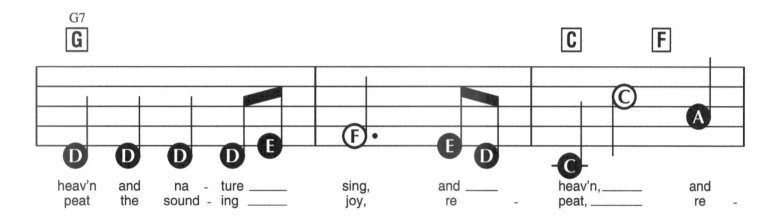

heav'n and na - ture _____ sing, and _____ heav'n, _____ and
peat the sound - ing _____ joy, and re - peat, _____ re -

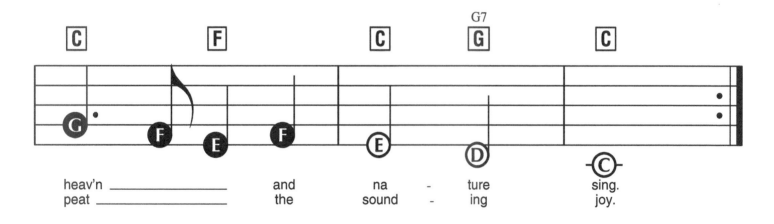

heav'n _____ and na - ture sing.
peat _____ the sound - ing joy.

Additional Lyrics

3. No more let sins and sorrows grow
Nor thorns infest the ground;
He comes to make His blessings flow
Far as the curse is found.

4. He rules the world with truth and grace
And makes the nations prove
The glories of His righteousness
And wonders of His love.

Last Christmas

Registration 1
Rhythm: Disco or 16 Beat

Words and Music by
George Michael

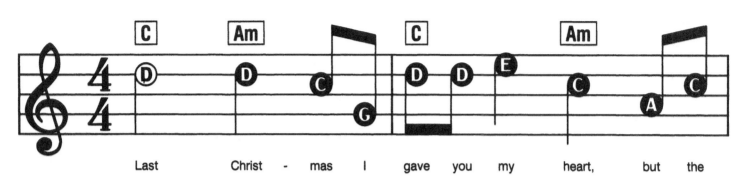

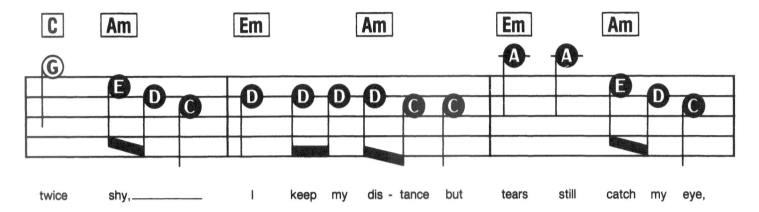

twice shy,_____ I keep my dis - tance but tears still catch my eye,

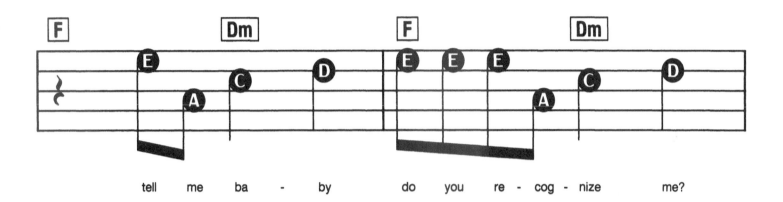

tell me ba - by do you re - cog - nize me?

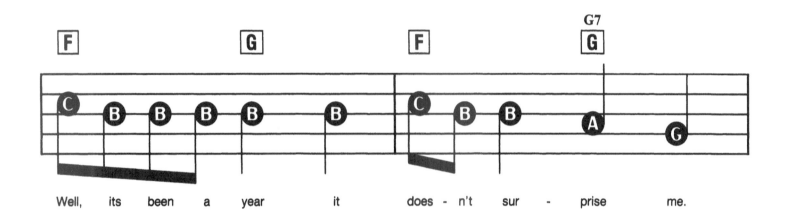

Well, its been a year it does - n't sur - prise me.

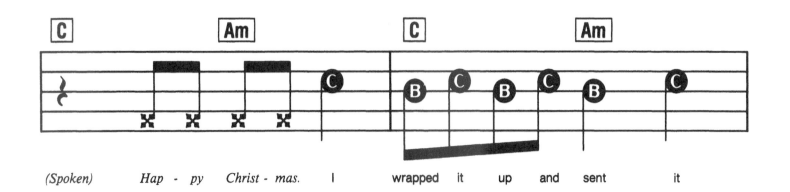

(Spoken) *Hap - py Christ - mas.* I wrapped it up and sent it

(Spoken) May - be next year I'll give it to some - one, I'll

give it to some - one spe - cial, spe - cial,_____

some - one,_____

Repeat and Fade

G7

some - one I'll give it to some - one, I'll give it to some - one

Additional Lyrics

A crowded room, friends with tired eyes.
I'm hiding from you and your soul of ice.
My God, I thought you were someone to rely on.
Me, I guess I was a shoulder to cry on.
A face on a lover with a fire in his heart,
A man under cover but you tore me apart.
Oo, now I've found a new love.
You'll never fool me again.

Let It Snow! Let It Snow! Let It Snow!

Registration 2
Rhythm: Fox Trot or Swing

Words by Sammy Cahn
Music by Jule Styne

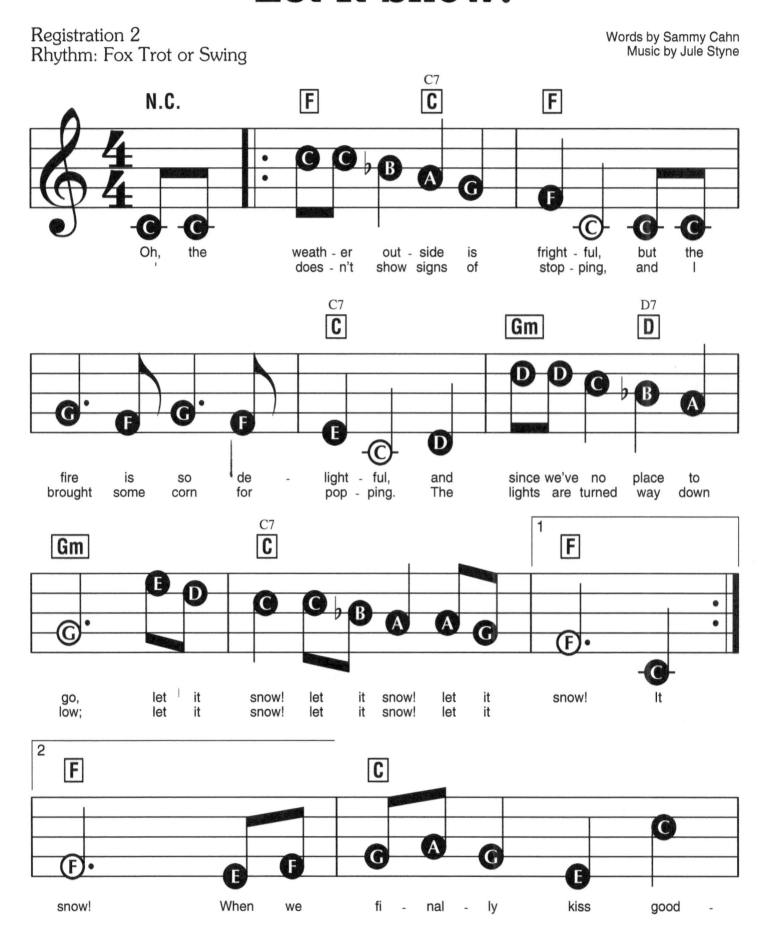

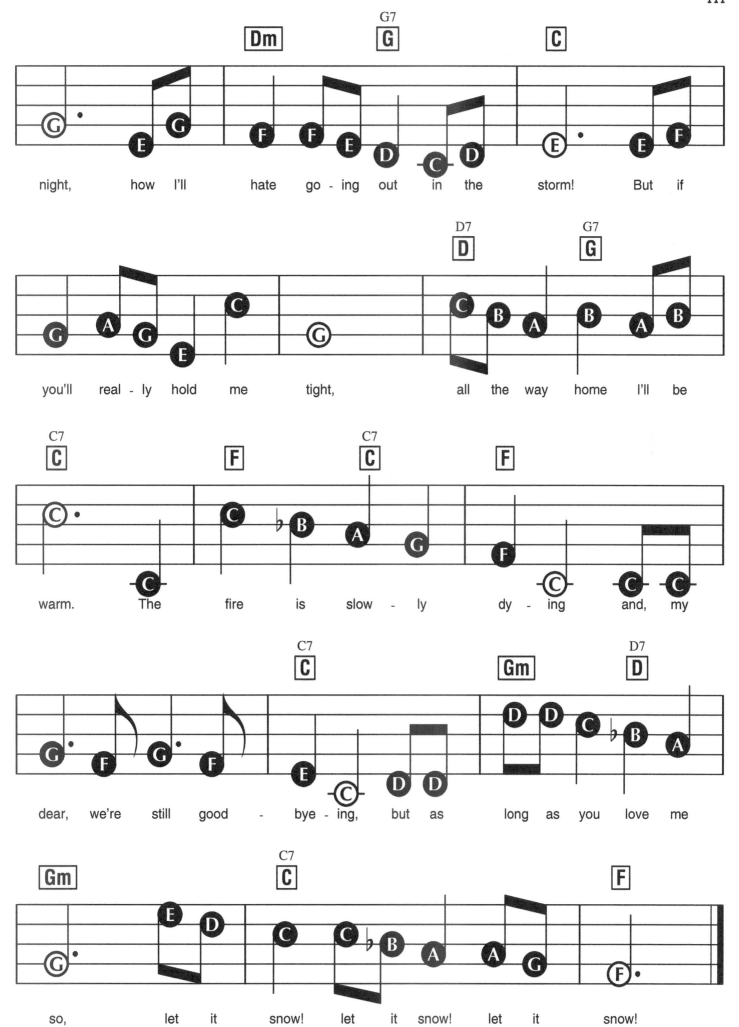

Mistletoe and Holly

Registration 2
Rhythm: Swing

Words and Music by Frank Sinatra,
Dok Stanford and Henry Sanicola

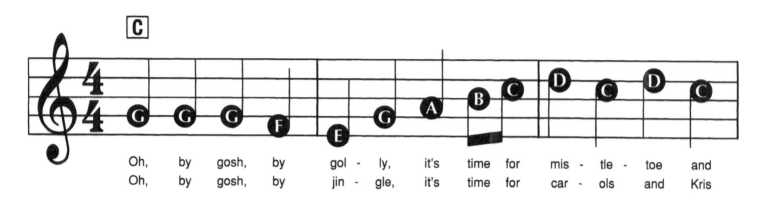

Oh, by gosh, by gol - ly, it's time for mis - tle - toe and
Oh, by gosh, by jin - gle, it's time for car - ols and Kris

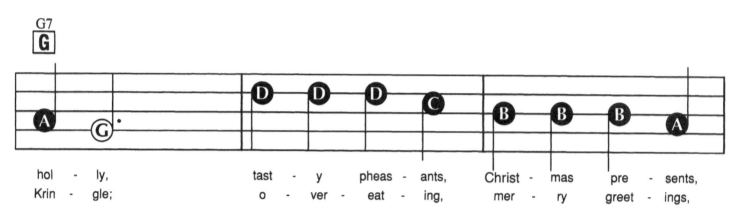

hol - ly, tast - y pheas - ants, Christ - mas pre - sents,
Krin - gle; o - ver - eat - ing, mer - ry greet - ings,

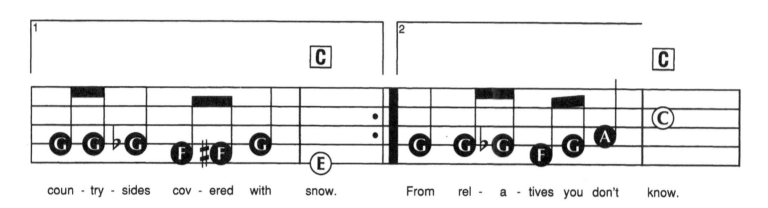

coun - try - sides cov - ered with snow. From rel - a - tives you don't know.

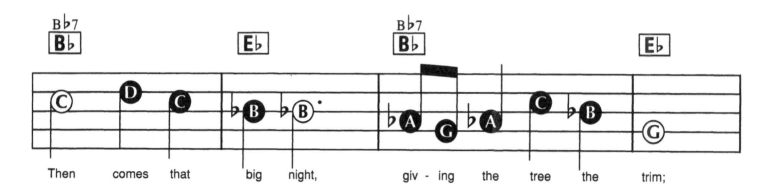

Then comes that big night, giv - ing the tree the trim;

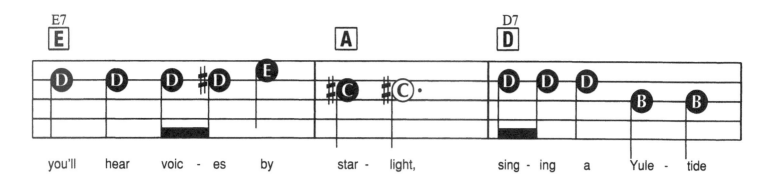

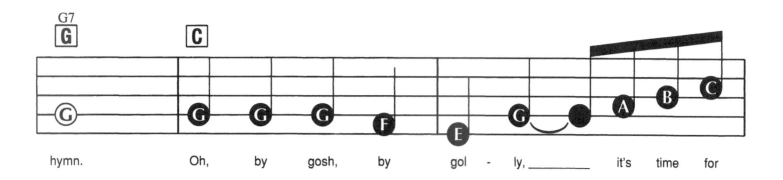

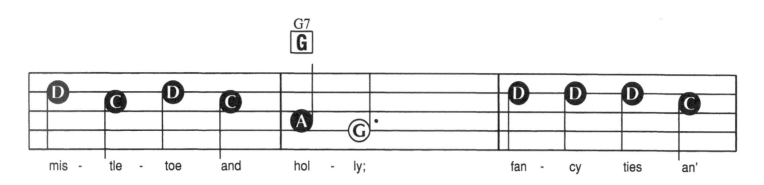

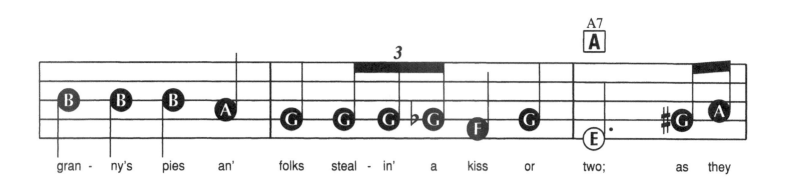

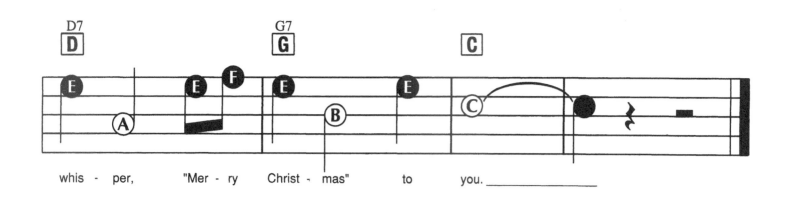

O Holy Night

Registration 6
Rhythm: None

French Words by Placide Cappeau
English Words by John S. Dwight
Music by Adolphe Adam

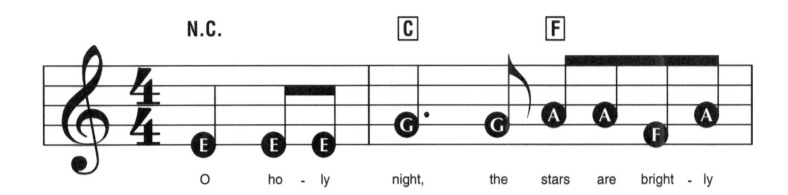

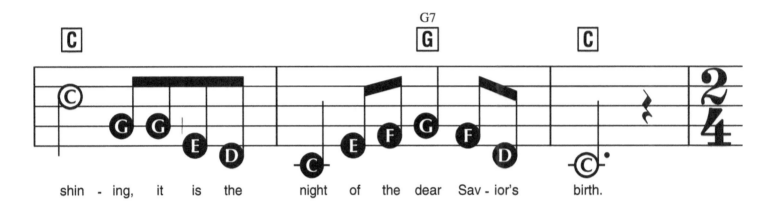

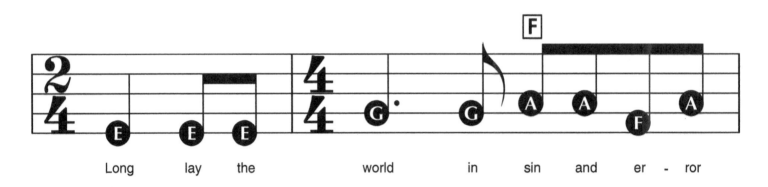

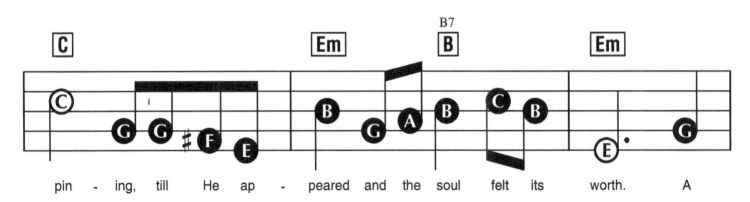

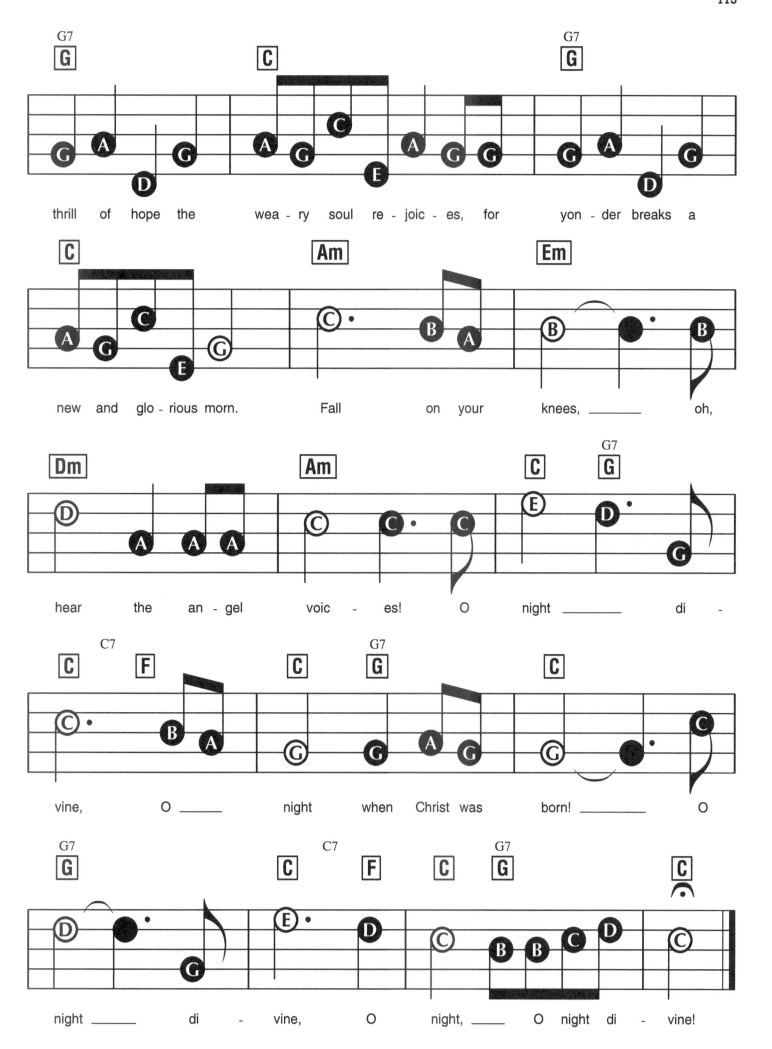

O Little Town of Bethlehem

Registration 1
Rhythm: Fox Trot

Words by Phillips Brooks
Music by Lewis H. Redner

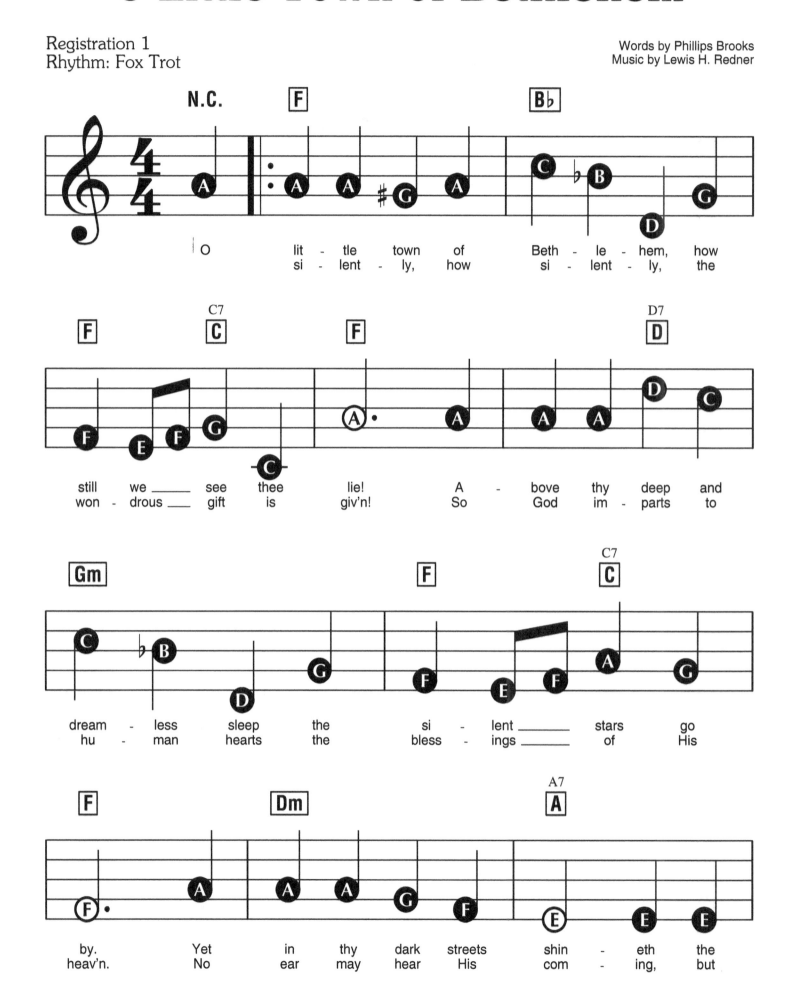

117

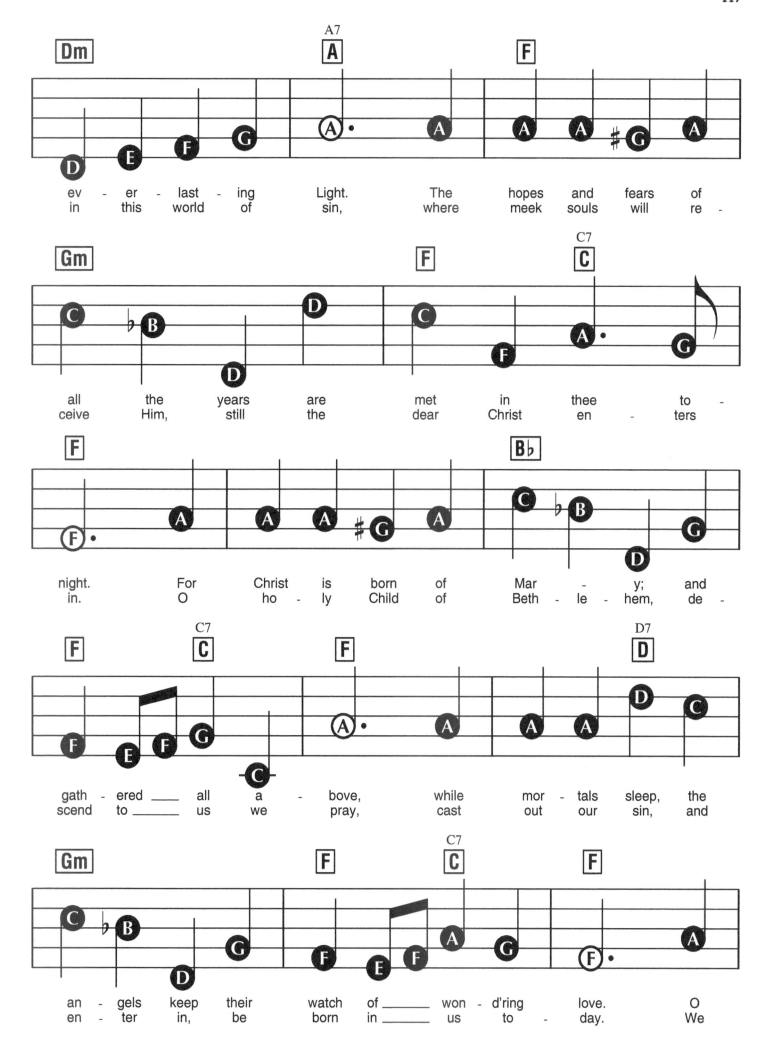

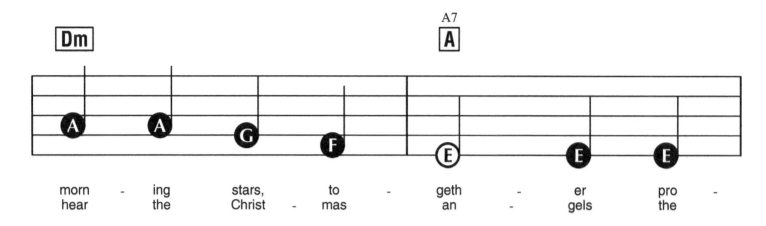

morn - ing stars, to - geth - er pro -
hear the Christ - mas an - gels pro the

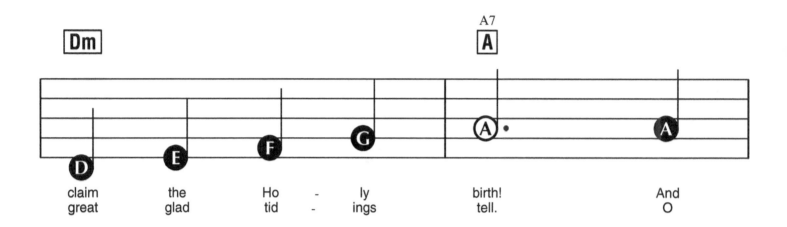

claim the Ho - ly birth! And
great the glad tid - ings tell. O

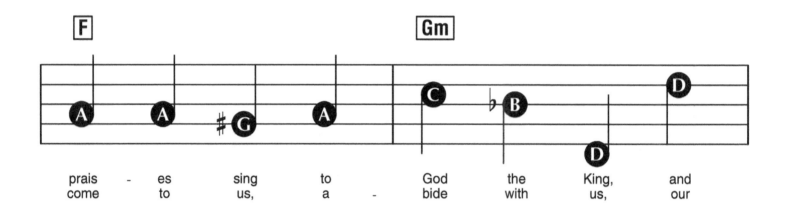

prais - es sing to God the King, and
come to us, a - bide with us, and our

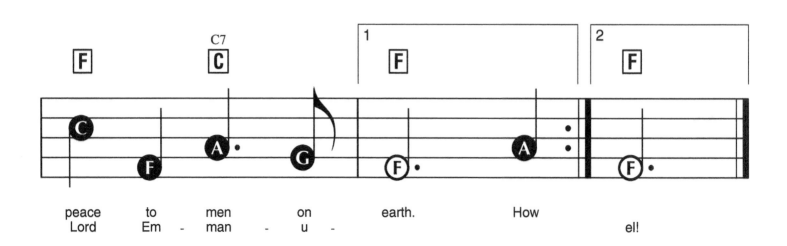

peace to men on earth. How
Lord to Em - man - u - el!

Please Come Home for Christmas

Registration 2
Rhythm: Slow Rock or Fifties Ballad

Words and Music by Charles Brown
and Gene Redd

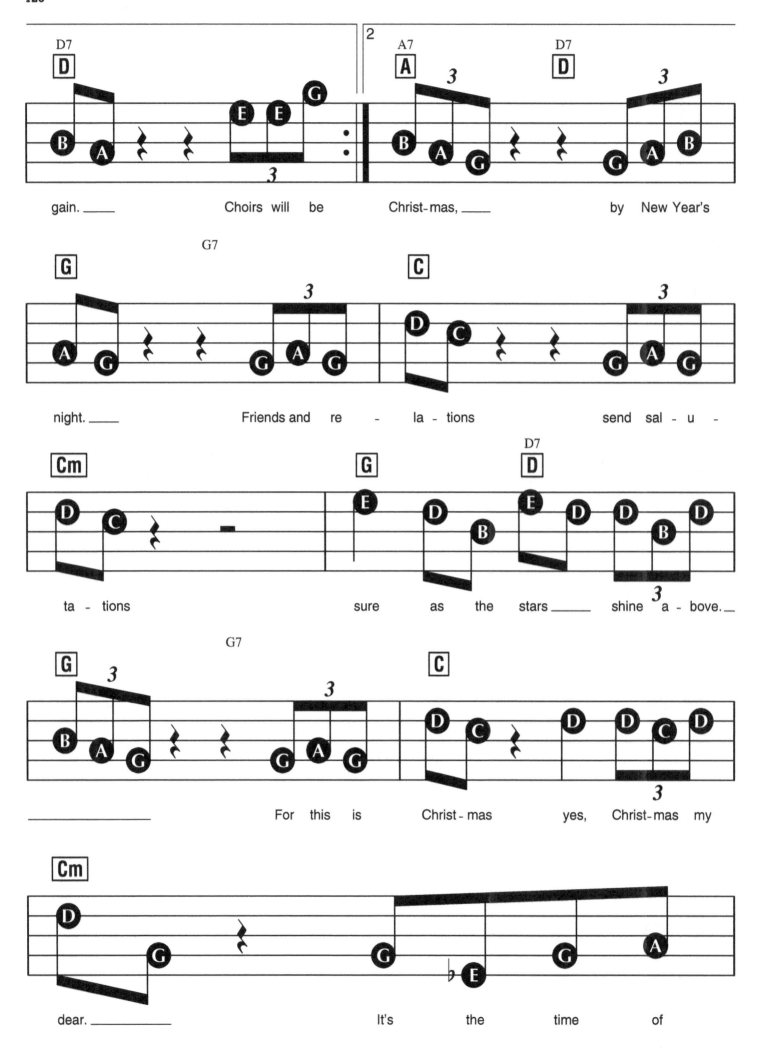

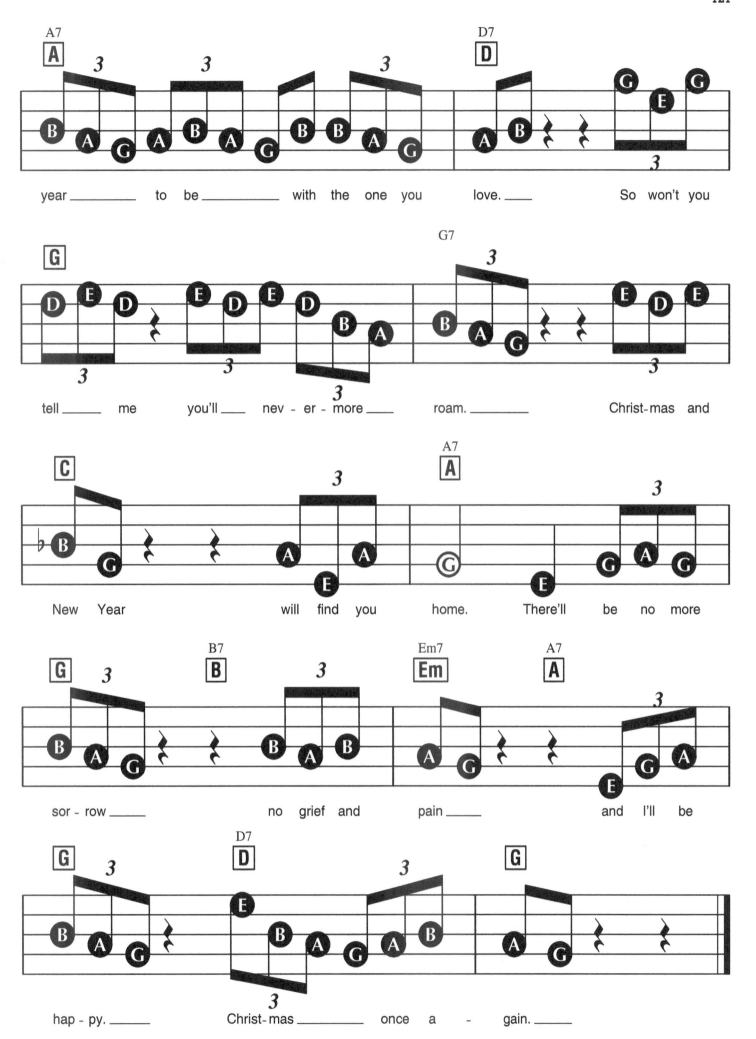

Rudolph the Red-Nosed Reindeer

Registration 4
Rhythm: Fox Trot or Swing

Music and Lyrics by
Johnny Marks

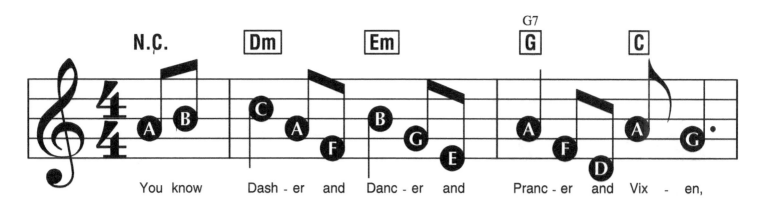

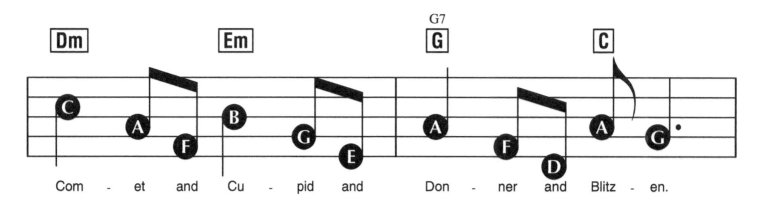

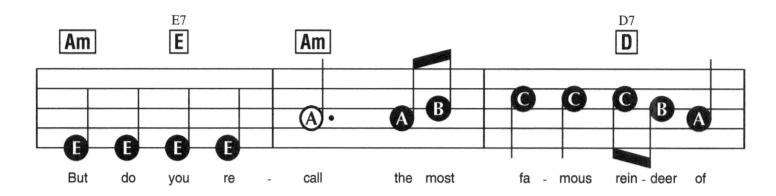

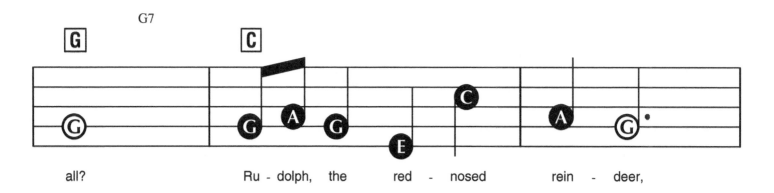

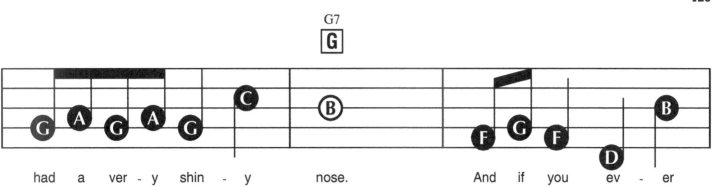

had a ver - y shin - y nose. And if you ev - er

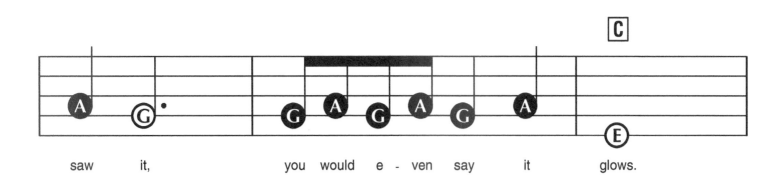

saw it, you would e - ven say it glows.

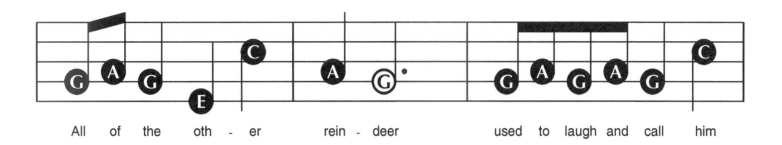

All of the oth - er rein - deer used to laugh and call him

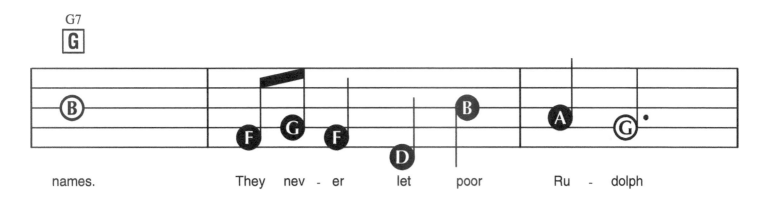

names. They nev - er let poor Ru - dolph

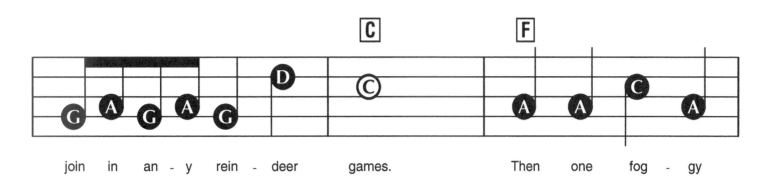

join in an - y rein - deer games. Then one fog - gy

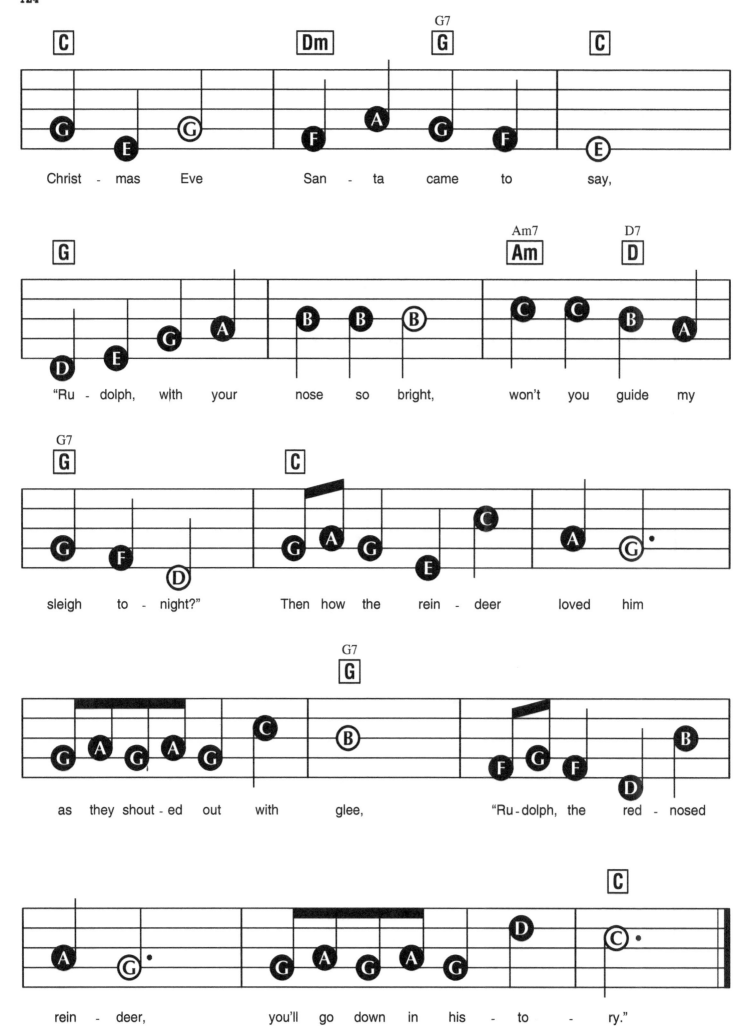

Santa, Bring My Baby Back
(To Me)

Registration 5
Rhythm: March

Words and Music by Claude DeMetrius
and Aaron Schroeder

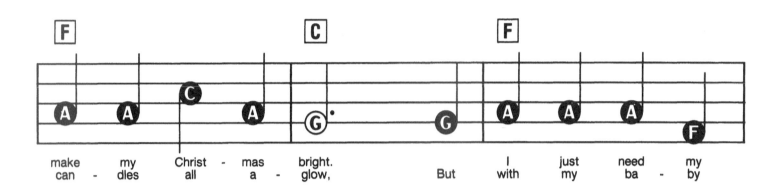

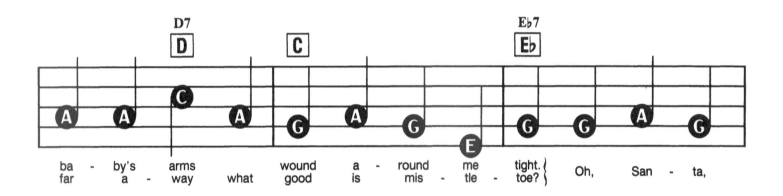

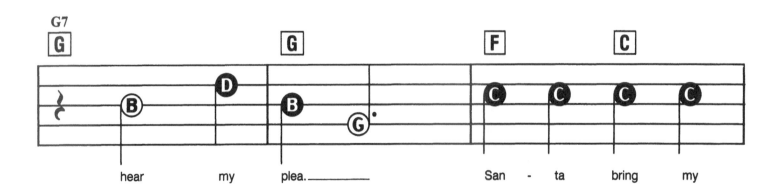

126

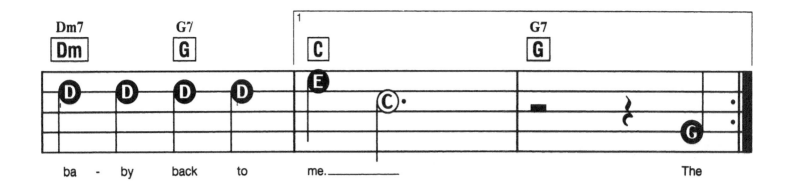

ba - by   back   to   me._____   The

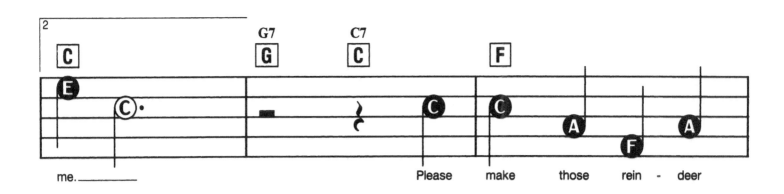

me._____   Please   make   those   rein - deer

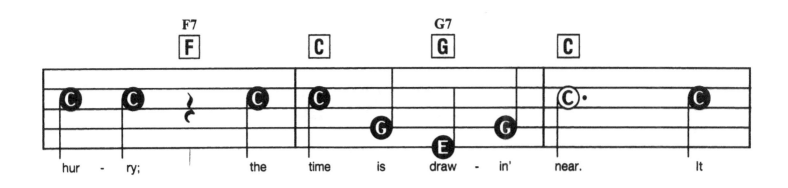

hur - ry;   the   time   is   draw - in'   near.   It

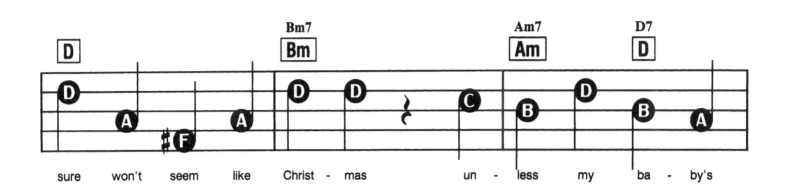

sure   won't   seem   like   Christ - mas   un - less   my   ba - by's

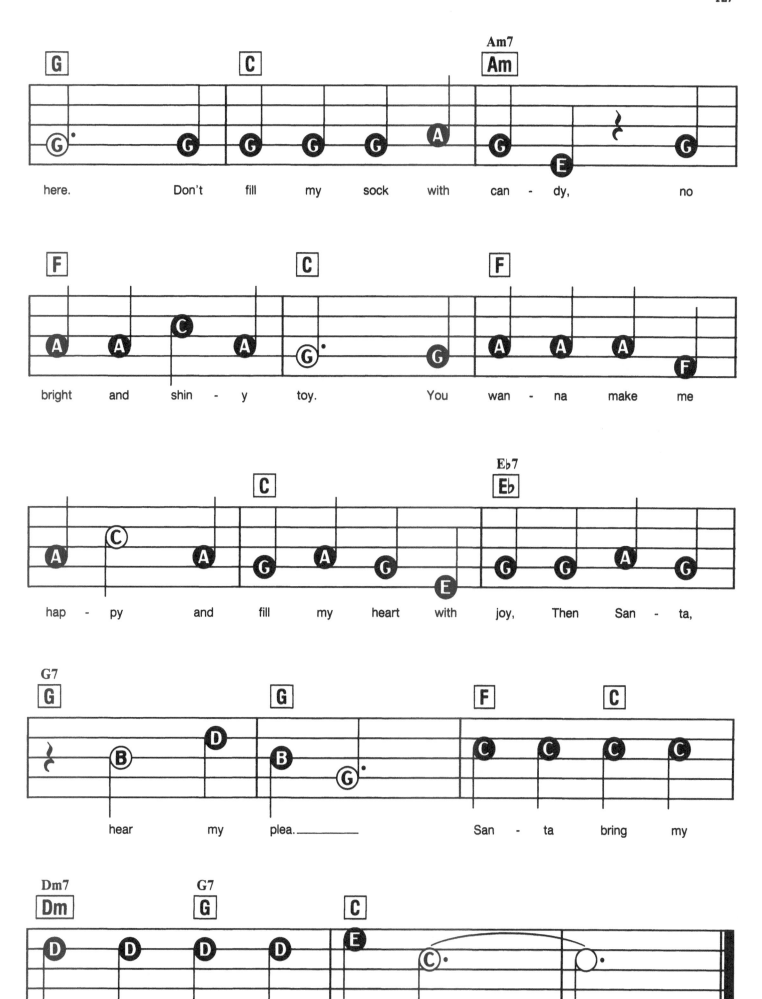

Santa Claus Is Comin' to Town

Registration 3
Rhythm: Swing or Big Band

Words by Haven Gillespie
Music by J. Fred Coots

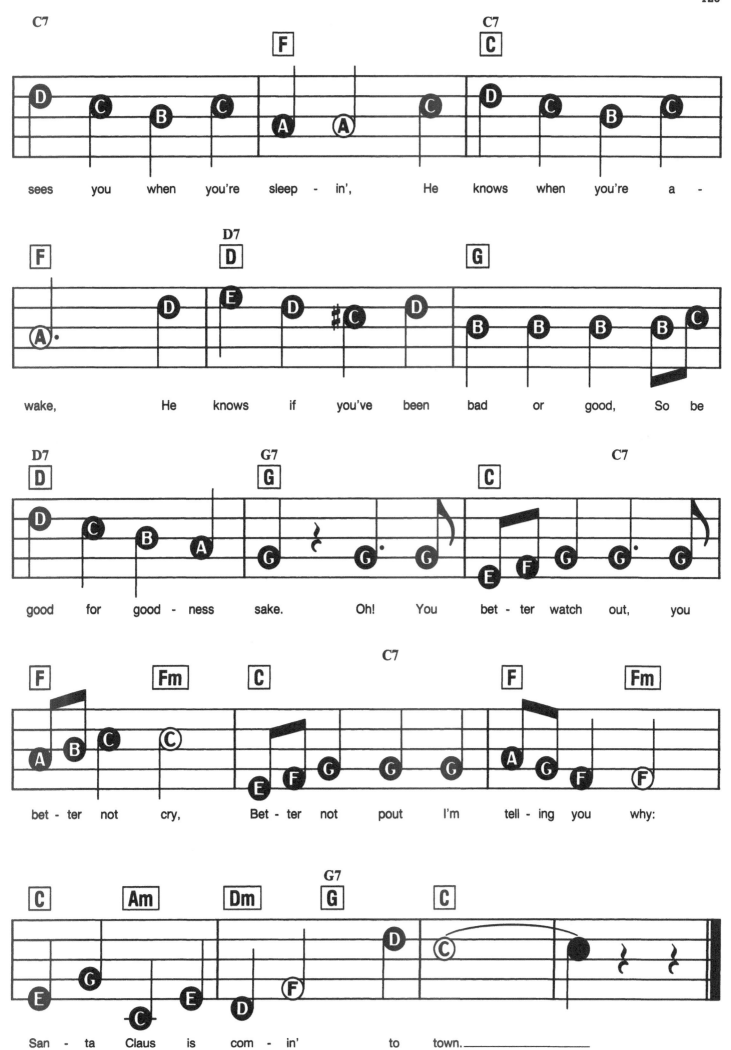

Silent Night

Registration 1
Rhythm: Waltz

Words by Joseph Mohr
Translated by John F. Young
Music by Franz X. Grüber

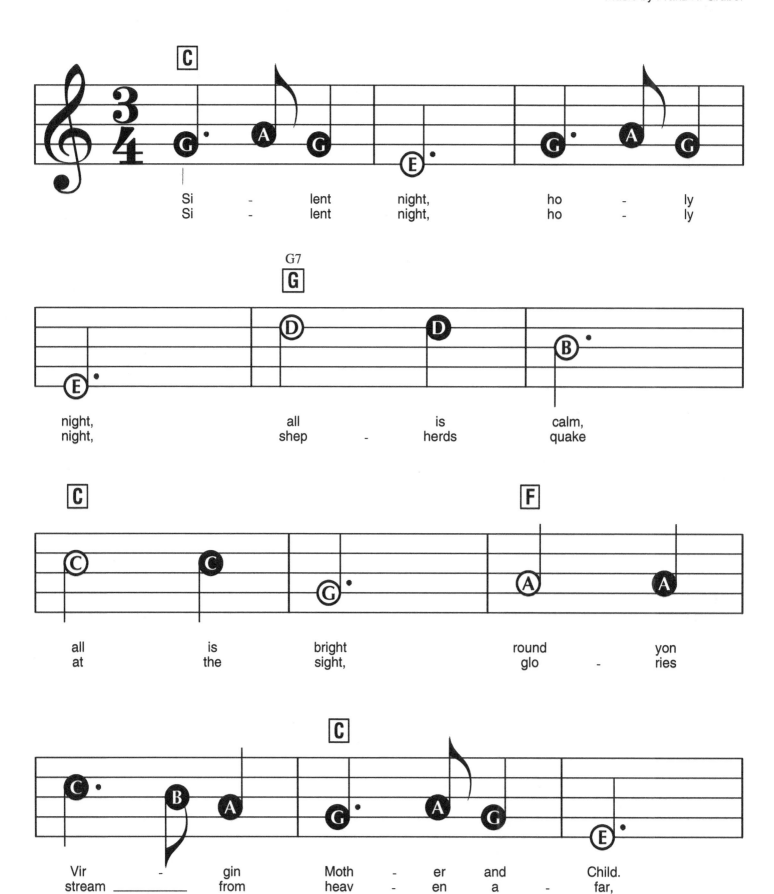

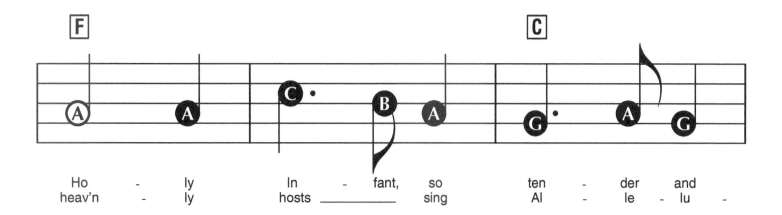

Ho - ly In - fant, so ten - der and
heav'n - ly hosts _____ sing Al - le - lu -

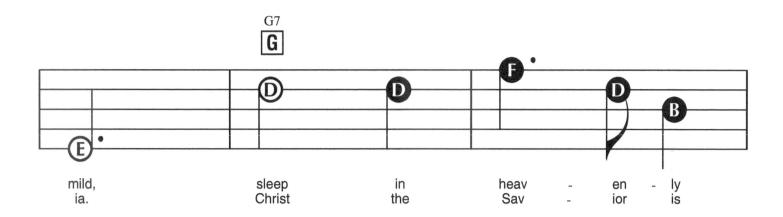

G7

mild, sleep in heav - en - ly
ia. Christ in the Sav - ior is

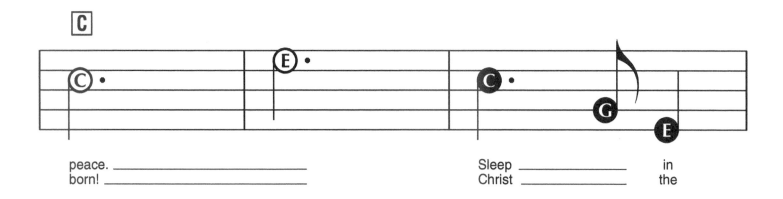

peace. _____
born! _____   Sleep _____ in
                               Christ _____ the

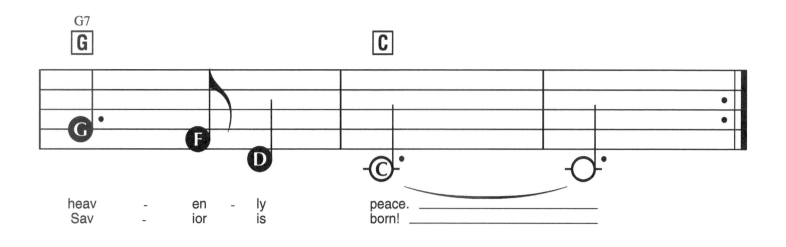

G7   C

heav - en - ly peace. _____
Sav - ior is born! _____

Silver Bells
from the Paramount Picture THE LEMON DROP KID

Registration 7
Rhythm: Waltz

Words and Music by Jay Livingston
and Ray Evans

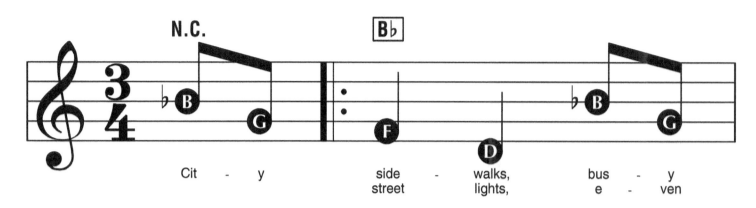

Cit - y | side - walks, bus - y
| street lights, e - ven

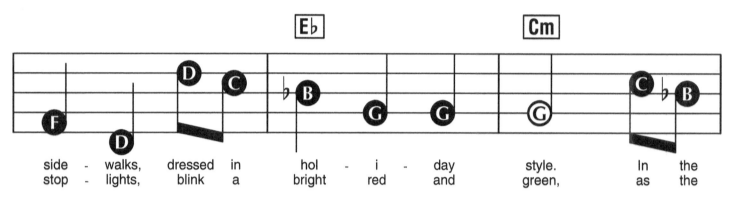

side - walks, dressed in hol - i - day style. In the
stop - lights, blink a bright red and green, as the

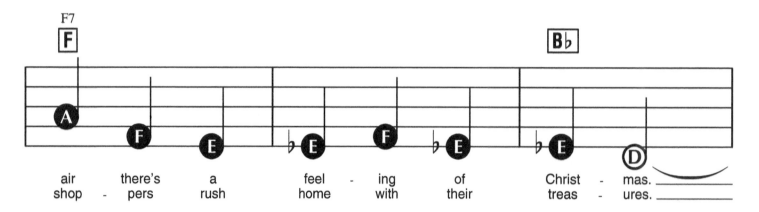

air there's a feel - ing of Christ - mas.
shop - pers rush home with their treas - ures.

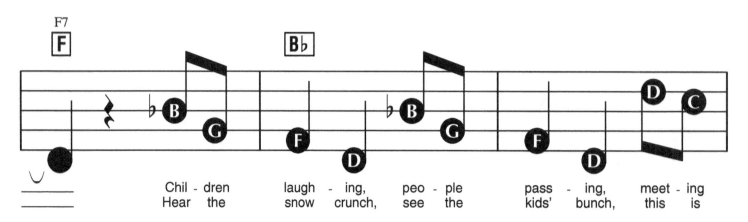

Chil - dren laugh - ing, peo - ple pass - ing, meet - ing
Hear the snow crunch, see the kids' bunch, this is

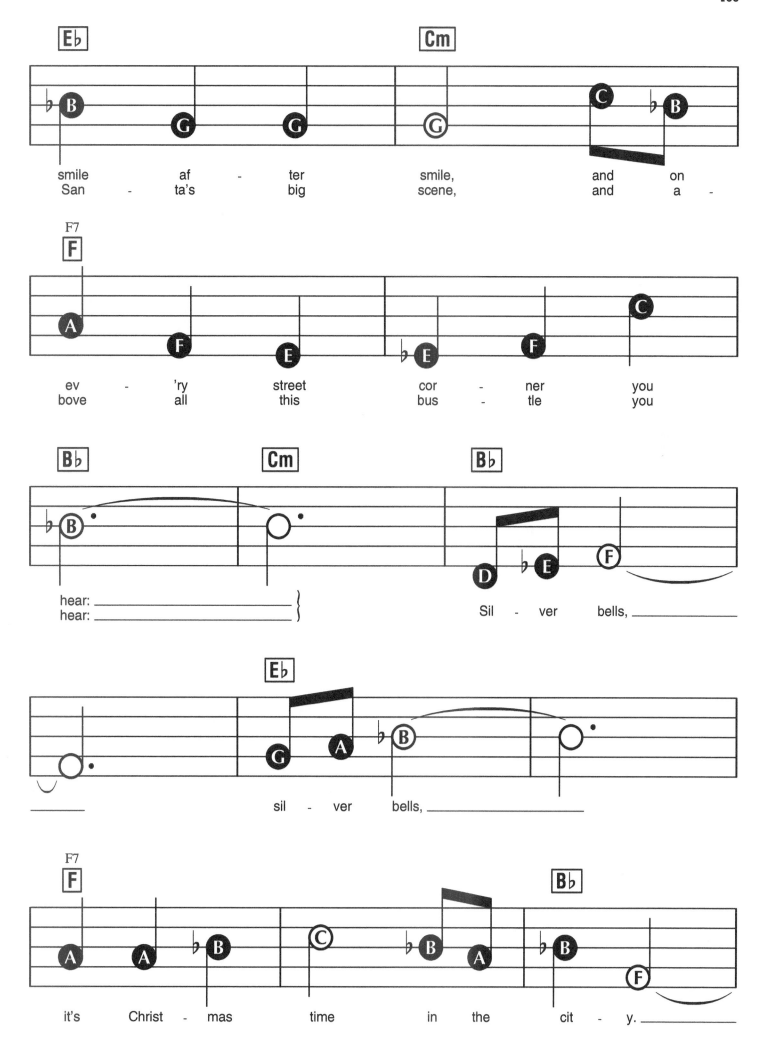

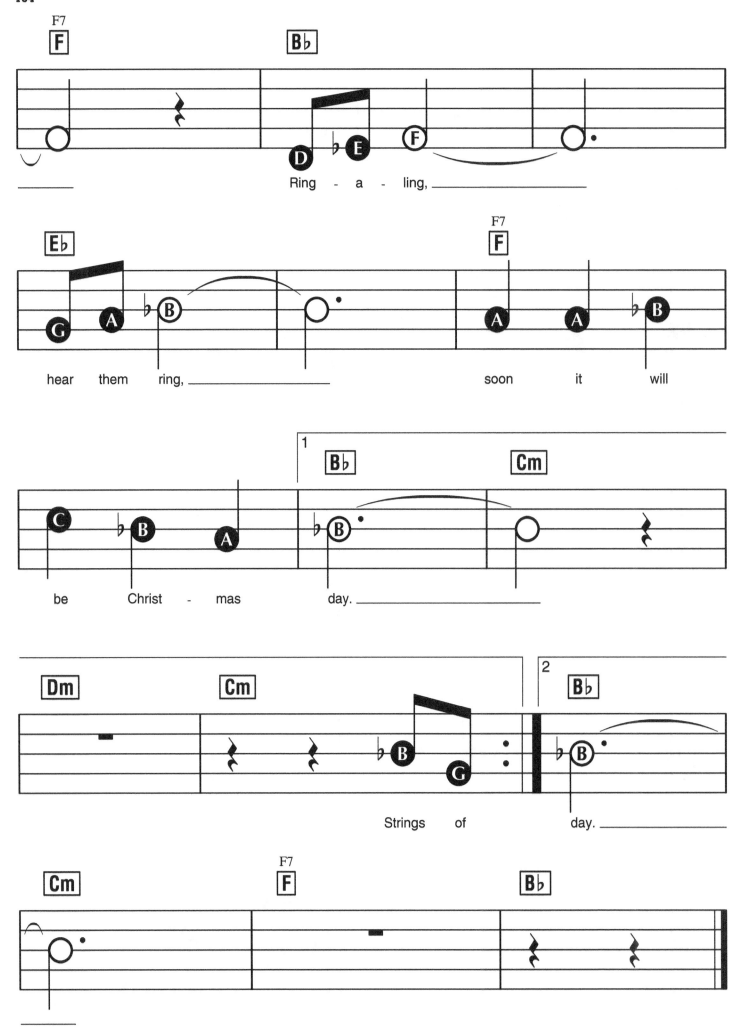

Wonderful Christmastime

Registration 3
Rhythm: Fox Trot

Words and Music by
Paul McCartney

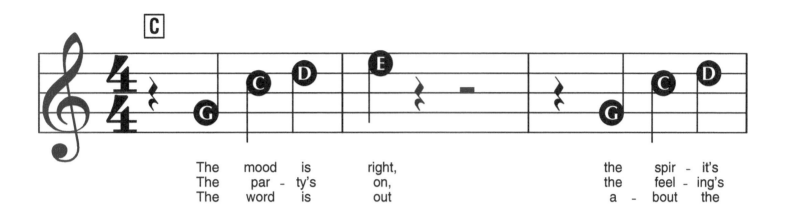

The mood is right, the spir - it's
The par - ty's on, the feel - ing's
The word is out a - bout the

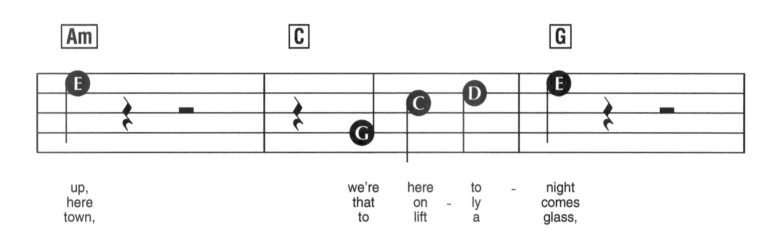

up, we're here to - night
here that on - ly comes
town, to lift a glass,

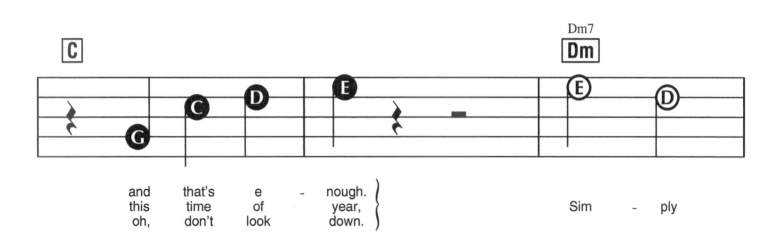

and that's e - nough.
this time of year, Sim - ply
oh, don't look down.

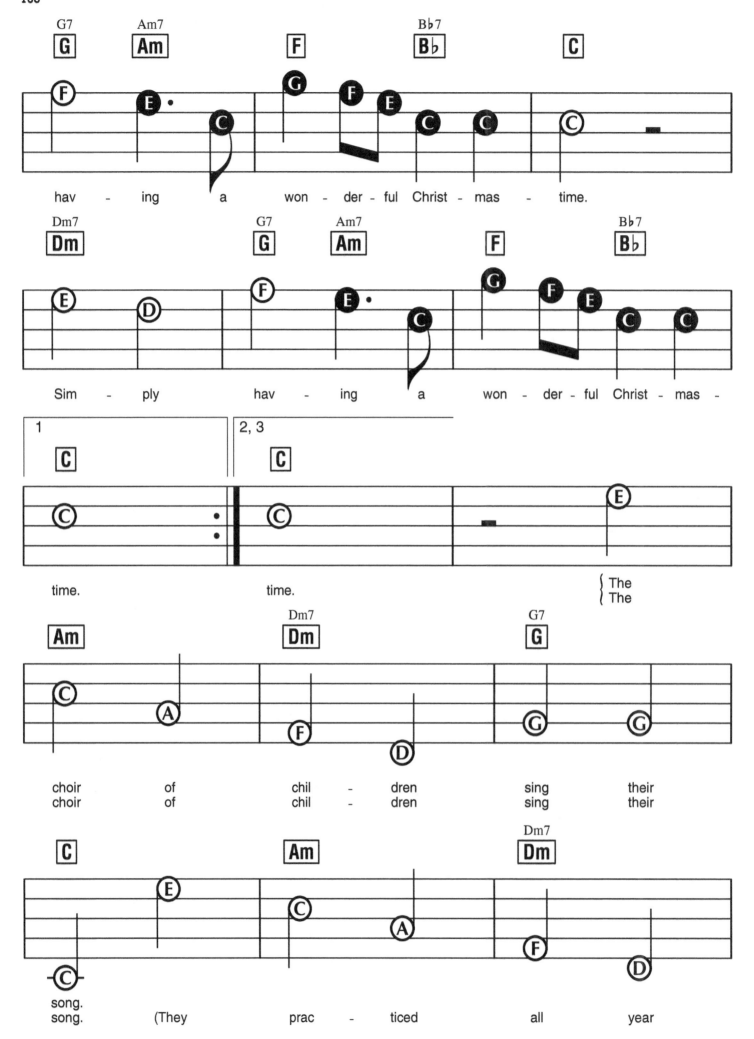

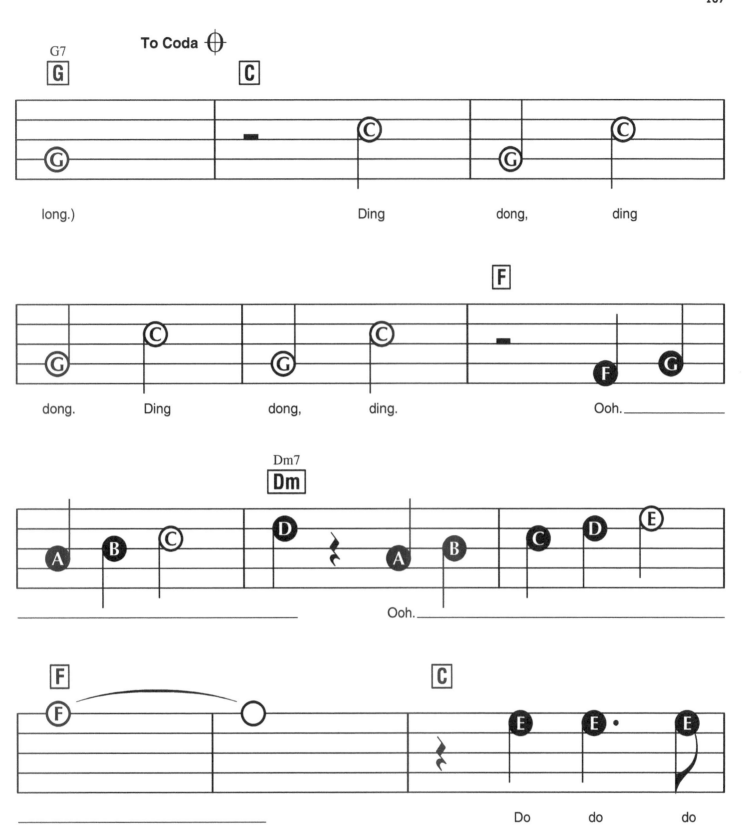

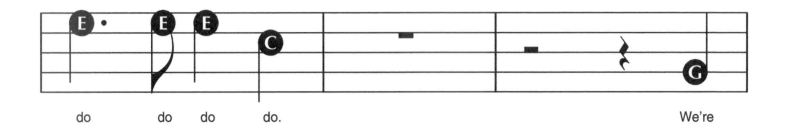

138

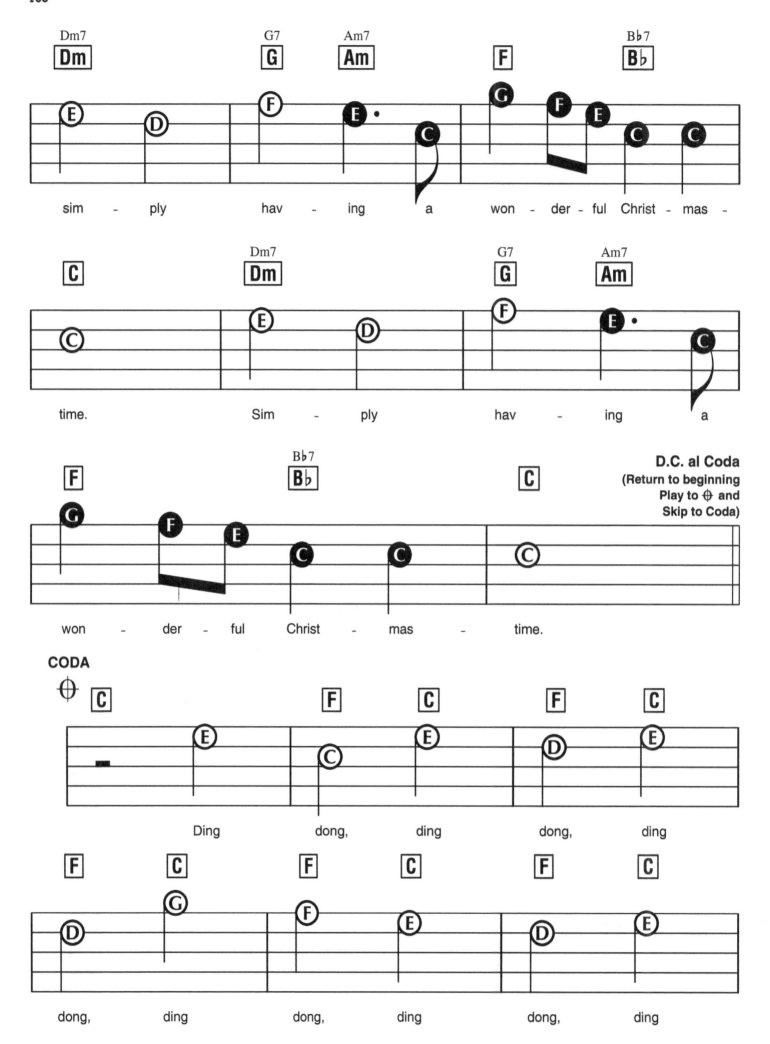

139

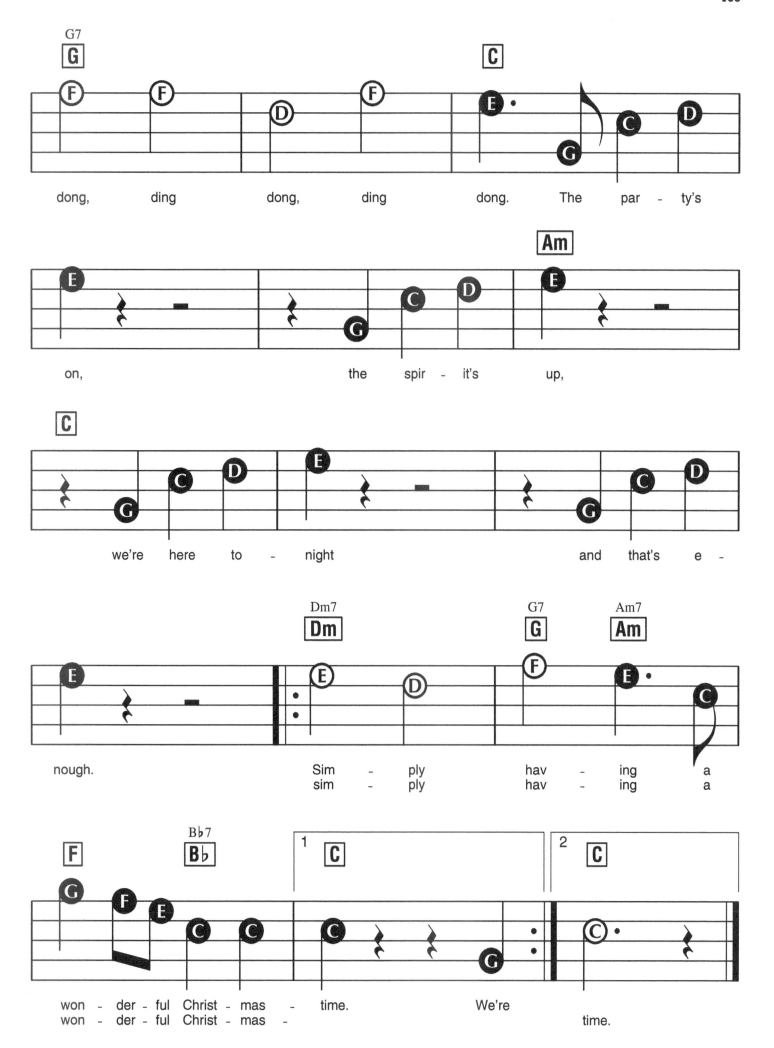

We Wish You a Merry Christmas

Registration 4
Rhythm: None

Traditional English Folksong

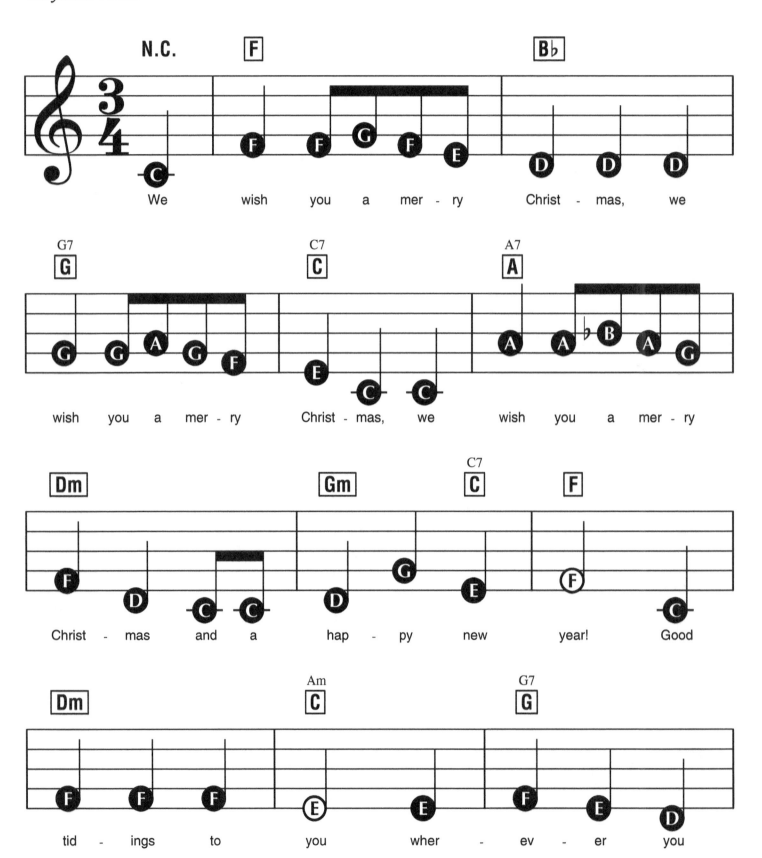

141

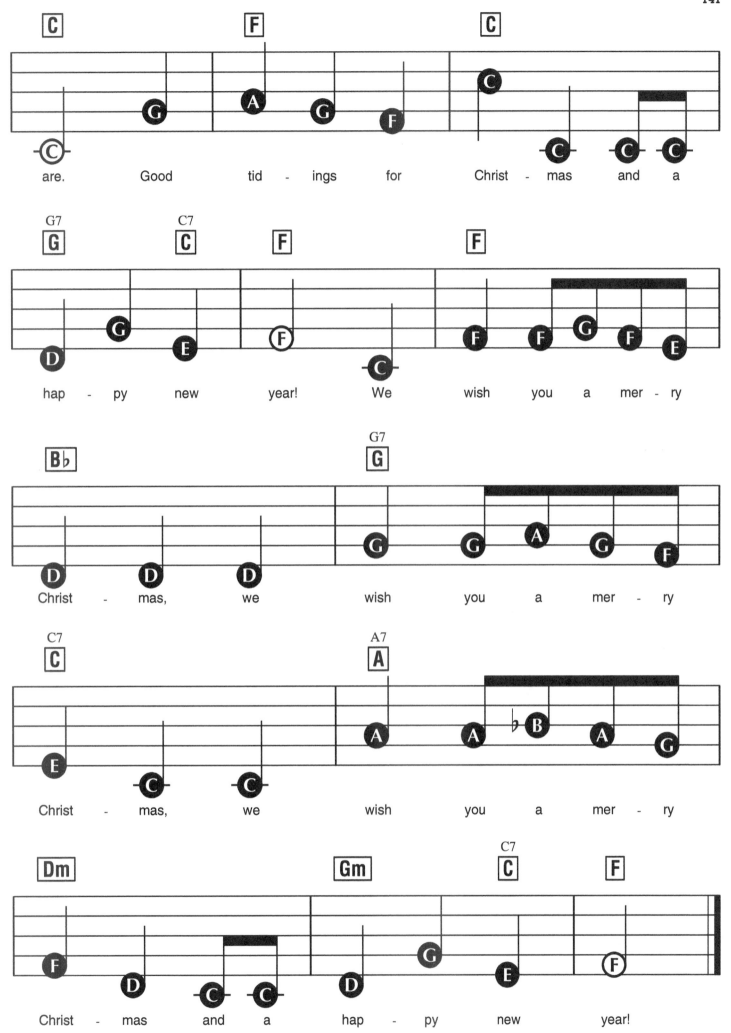

Registration Guide

- Match the Registration number on the song to the corresponding numbered category below. Select and activate an instrumental sound available on your instrument.

- Choose an automatic rhythm appropriate to the mood and style of the song. (Consult your Owner's Guide for proper operation of automatic rhythm features.)

- Adjust the tempo and volume controls to comfortable settings.

Registration

1	Mellow	Flutes, Clarinet, Oboe, Flugel Horn, Trombone, French Horn, Organ Flutes
2	Ensemble	Brass Section, Sax Section, Wind Ensemble, Full Organ, Theater Organ
3	Strings	Violin, Viola, Cello, Fiddle, String Ensemble, Pizzicato, Organ Strings
4	Guitars	Acoustic/Electric Guitars, Banjo, Mandolin, Dulcimer, Ukulele, Hawaiian Guitar
5	Mallets	Vibraphone, Marimba, Xylophone, Steel Drums, Bells, Celesta, Chimes
6	Liturgical	Pipe Organ, Hand Bells, Vocal Ensemble, Choir, Organ Flutes
7	Bright	Saxophones, Trumpet, Mute Trumpet, Synth Leads, Jazz/Gospel Organs
8	Piano	Piano, Electric Piano, Honky Tonk Piano, Harpsichord, Clavi
9	Novelty	Melodic Percussion, Wah Trumpet, Synth, Whistle, Kazoo, Perc. Organ
10	Bellows	Accordion, French Accordion, Mussette, Harmonica, Pump Organ, Bagpipes